Group
Treatment
for Adult
Survivors
of Abuse

Interpersonal Violence:
The Practice Series
Jon R. Conte, Series Editor

Interpersonal Violence: The Practice Series is devoted to mental health, social service, and allied professionals who confront daily the problem of interpersonal violence. It is hoped that the knowledge, professional experience, and high standards of practice offered by the authors of these volumes may lead to the end of interpersonal violence.

In this series...

Group Treatment for Adult Survivors of Abuse
A Manual for Practitioners

Laura Pistone Webb
James Leehan

Foreword by Christine A. Courtois

Interpersonal Violence:
The Practice Series

SAGE Publications
International Educational and Professional Publisher
Thousand Oaks   London   New Delhi

For information address:

SAGE Publications, Inc.
2455 Teller Road
Thousand Oaks, California 91320
E-mail: order@sagepub.com

SAGE Publications Ltd.
6 Bonhill Street
London EC2A 4PU
United Kingdom

SAGE Publications India Pvt. Ltd.
M-32 Market
Greater Kailash I
New Delhi 110 048 India

Printed in the United States of America

Library of Congress Cataloging-in-Publication Data

Webb, Laura Pistone.
   Group treatment for adult survivors of abuse: a manual for
practitioners / Laura Pistone Webb, James Leehan.
       p.   cm.—(Interpersonal violence: the practice series; v. 14)
   Includes bibliographical references and index.
   ISBN 0-8039-5171-X (acid-free paper).—ISBN 0-8039-5172-8
(pbk.: acid-free paper).
       1. Adult child abuse victims. 2. Group psychotherapy. I. Leehan,
James. III. Title. Series.
   RC569.5.C55W42   1996
   616.85'822390651—dc20   96-10020

This book is printed on acid-free paper.

96 97 98 99 10 9 8 7 6 5 4 3 2 1

Sage Production Editor: *Vicki Baker*   Sage Typesetter: *Marion Warren*

This book is dedicated to the many brave adults who have participated in the groups that we have led over the years. Their courage has been an inspiration, and their persistence and determination in healing the wounds of their childhoods have taught us much about the resilience of the human spirit. They have provided powerful role models and given much hope to countless others. They are more than survivors, they are victors!

Contents

Foreword

In the late 1970s and throughout the 1980s, studies of child abuse documented its widespread prevalence and impact on American society. These studies further documented that child abuse is not unitary; rather, it has many patterns of occurrence and many varieties, including physical, sexual, spiritual, and psychological/emotional maltreatment, in addition to deprivation and neglect. Unfortunately, these various forms of abuse are not mutually exclusive, and one type often overlaps with or occurs in conjunction with others. A major strength of this book is its holistic orientation to the problem of child abuse and its effects. It acknowledges the variation and the overlap and recommends a treatment strategy that is encompassing rather than restrictive to only one type.

Abuse is now identified as a traumatic stressor for the child victim with high potential for a range of damaging consequences. A sizable number of victims suffer both initial and long-term consequences, many of which are severe enough to interfere with personal maturation and to persist across the life span. This book addresses the longer term effects of abuse and sets out both the characteristics and needs of adults abused as children. It describes a specific treatment modality—community-based coed group treatment organized by a male-female cotherapy team—that has proven successful in assisting many adult survivors with neutralizing or reversing the effects of their early experiences of abuse.

A model such as the one described in this book is very much needed in this day and age. The unprecedented societal acknowledgment of the prevalence of abuse has allowed large numbers of adult survivors to uncover their abuse and to seek treatment for its effects at a time when, unfortunately, mental health budgets and resources are decreasing and managed care efforts are intensifying. These societal and economic forces require the development of more innovative, cost-effective, efficient forms of treatment. Group models, although certainly not superseding individual therapy, nevertheless provide some affordable as well as effective alternatives.

Additionally, groups are especially important in healing the effects of victimization. Abuse most often occurs in isolation and secrecy, causing shame responses in the victim. It is often perpetrated by someone of personal significance to the child and involves betrayal of the relationship, resulting in mistrust of others and difficulty with intimacy. Groups have great therapeutic value as a context in which to destigmatize the effects of abuse, interact with peers who experienced similar events, and give and receive feedback and assistance. Groups have a much higher potential than does individual treatment for the observation of the members' relational patterns while simultaneously offering a forum for feedback and for trying out new behaviors and interactions.

From my perspective, this book's most substantive contribution is in the articulation of the advantages and complications of group treatment for this specialized population, as well as strategies for management and containment. Group leaders need guidelines and information that are not taught in standard curricula and are not widely available otherwise. Many clinicians have had to learn from their mistakes, a process that can be costly to them and to the clients they serve. Stories of group "disasters" abound among therapists in the abuse survivors' field, disasters that are largely due to the lack of knowledge about the population and the chaining effect (Leehan

and Webb call these the complications of such grou
issues can have when survivors interact in a grou'
make special demands and require special dedicatic.
so aptly described by the authors, themselves the veterans o.
merous group sessions and cycles.

The authors begin with a detailed description of the personal and interpersonal/relational effects of abuse, many of which get played out in the dynamics of the group's interactions. For example, mistrust of others and suspiciousness regarding their motives characterize many survivors' worldview. They therefore enter group from this stance, which they play out to a greater or lesser degree, consciously or unconsciously, with others who have similar difficulties. Group leaders must have a thorough understanding of these effects and how they might influence group dynamics in order to be able to structure and process group interaction. Such a knowledge base, along with a theoretical orientation that is derived from traumatic stress and relational models, assists the clinicians in understanding the issues and interactions and responding appropriately. Leaders must continuously seek to understand the traumatic roots of various reactions in order to promote understanding by all group members and to provide the opportunity to change feelings and relational patterns.

The authors wisely devote attention to the group leader, including the therapeutic stance necessary for running these groups, and strategies for self-care. The model described requires the leader to serve as a mentor at the same time that he or she is the object of strong projections and transference reactions from members because of being in a quasi-parental, authority figure role. The use of a male-female cotherapy team enlists these reactions and provides a therapeutic context for their resolution. The opportunity for healing is great, as are the demands on the therapists. The self-care attention and strategies are well warranted.

This book is optimistic in its orientation and offers hope to survivors of all forms of abuse that they can overcome the legacy of their past. This book was spawned from 15 years of experience and offers group leaders valuable insight into the functioning and utility of such a group model. The model is applicable in many clinical settings, particularly those that cannot provide long-term individual treatment, and seek viable alternatives to meet the needs of the population of adult survivors of abuse.

Christine A. Courtois

Preface

In February of 1978, the first group for adult survivors of child abuse and neglect (formerly called *grown-up abused children*) was formed at Cleveland State University. That initial group was co-led by a social service professor and a campus minister.

The professor had taught a class on child abuse. Following that class, several students approached her individually and shared the fact that they were former victims of abuse. For many of them, this was the first time they had discussed their abuse experience with anyone. They were surprised to learn that child abuse was not uncommon, for they believed that they were the only people to whom this had happened. The sense of isolation and fear they conveyed was profound.

This professor later shared these comments with a campus minister at the university. He had encountered a similar sense of secrecy and shame from individual counselees who finally had been able to discuss their abusive experience. As the two discussed the issue, it seemed appropriate to invite these various people to come together in a group to share their experiences and attempt to break down the sense of isolation. The students were approached individually with this idea, and, with a mixture of eagerness and reticence, most of them agreed to give it a try.

Although the first meeting began hesitantly, a great sense of relief soon pervaded the room as one after another, the students revealed their past experiences of abuse and their present struggles to overcome the fear and mistrust that seemed to rule their lives. This group continued to meet weekly for 6 months until graduation, jobs, and summer schedules forced an ending. In those few months, the members gained new friends, new insights into what had happened to them, new skills for developing and maintaining interpersonal relationships, and immeasurable relief from the guilt and isolation that had plagued them for years. They no longer perceived themselves as bad children who deserved the treatment they had received.

In the years since that first group, several others have been conducted. Members have participated for a few months or for several years—the longest any person participated was 5 years. The almost universal reaction of participants is that of relief and release as they are finally freed to discuss the deep, dark secret of their abusive past.

Many groups have been conducted in the Cleveland area since 1978. At one time, six different groups were meeting simultaneously. A previous version of this book, *Grown-Up Abused Children*, was planned originally to be a training manual for new group leaders. We have co-led groups together for 8 years, and Jim has led groups continuously since 1978.

For those of us who have become involved in the program as leaders, the experience has opened up a new appreciation of the complexity of child abuse. We have come to a new understanding of the wide range of effects that experience can have on the lives of those who have been subjected to it.

We are all aware of child abuse as a problem in our society. It has received increasing attention in the past 10 to 15 years as more and more incidents are being reported by physicians, social workers, teachers, and school counselors. The media are reporting incidents and examining causes. Programs are being developed to protect the child victims and to provide treatment for the abusive parents, many of whom were abused themselves.

Legislation has been enacted making it mandatory to report suspected incidents of child abuse. Child abuse hotlines have been established, and organizations such as Parents Anonymous have developed special programs to deal with the needs of abusive parents and teach them new parenting skills. Most mental health treatment centers now offer family counseling, and researchers have begun to study family dynamics and personality variables that seem related to spouse and child abuse.

However, even with this flurry of attention, until more recently, one part of the population related to the abuse problem has not received much attention—the adult survivors of child abuse. Each year, thousands of children in our society experience abuse in a variety of forms—physical, sexual, verbal, emotional, and neglect. And each year, thousands of these same children grow into adulthood and strive to develop meaningful relationships and satisfying adult lives. Unfortunately, these former victims of abuse carry with them many secret pains and frustrations, many unresolved fears, and a multitude of emotional wounds that have never healed and that seriously hinder their ability to function as mature, productive adults.

A common assumption in our society is that when a person moves into adulthood, the effects of his or her abusive background will disappear. The problem is over, and the child will "grow out of" or "get over" any difficulties or psychological disabilities caused by physical or sexual abuse or neglect. Survivors can seek out and receive individual therapy, but few, if any, groups or community programs are available to assist former victims in overcoming the effects of the abuse on their developmental process. And this dearth of treatment opportunities continues despite the growing understanding in the human service professions regarding the process of psychological development.

The fact that most abuse victims were deprived of many developmental opportunities and that they received clearly conflicting, contradictory, and even false messages about themselves must be accounted for in any kind of treatment. The impact of these experiences does not simply disappear or automatically diminish when one reaches adulthood.

The first part of this book provides working definitions of the various types of abuse and describes the major, recurring problems faced by those who were abused. These problems frequently hinder or preclude survivors' abilities to function in a happy, healthy, and productive manner. Although these problems are not unique in and of themselves, for these adults, the cumulative effect of their negative childhood experiences makes the issues more intense. If we view these problems as an interrelated and self-perpetuating cluster and place them in a developmental framework with a history of abuse and neglect, the need for treatment of the whole becomes clear. As one of these adults once stated, "When I stopped trying to deal with each issue one at a time and realized that they were all linked together and tied to my abusive past, it became easier to understand what I was up against and what I needed."

It is our belief, and the belief of the many people who have worked with groups for adult survivors in the past few years, that much more needs to be done to develop an understanding of and treatment modalities for the long-term effects of child abuse and neglect. In the 10 years since publication of an earlier version of this book, much research has been conducted, and theoretical frameworks for understanding and treating the effects of abuse are being developed. More and more, it is becoming apparent that a "treatment of choice" for adult survivors includes some form of group experience in conjunction with individual therapy.

A main focus of this book, then, is to describe a group treatment strategy and discuss why and how it works. We have found this intervention to be very effective when used by itself or in conjunction with individual therapy.

The specific goals for these groups will be described. Unique characteristics of the groups will be highlighted, including how they differ from other forms of group psychotherapy. In particular, the role of group leaders and special problems of transference and countertransference will be explored. Case studies and examples are interspersed throughout the text to show the relationship between the abuse experience, the problems of adulthood, and the therapeutic value of these support groups. In addition, after many years of working with adult survivors, we have become aware of the potential for therapists to experience secondary posttraumatic stress. Thus, a chapter on therapist self-care has been included.

We hope that these materials will assist professionals in developing forms of treatment for the many child abuse victims in our society who have had the good fortune to survive into adulthood. We hope that the adult years of these former victims can be less painful than their childhood, and that they can become contented and productive members of our society.

Many people and organizations have helped to make this book possible. The first person who must be thanked is Professor Elizabeth Carmichael, whose sensitive presentation of the problem of child abuse in her social service class enabled her students to discuss their own experiences with her. Her responsiveness to their needs really motivated the formation of the first group. Dr. Christine Courtois worked with the second group while she was at the Counseling Center at Cleveland State University, and her insights were crucial in the formulation of the initial analysis of individual needs and group process concerns. We are grateful for her continued support and her willingness to write the foreword to this edition. We would like to thank reviewers Tom Roesler, MD, of the National Jewish Center for Immunology and Respiratory Medicine, and Julie Lipovsky, PhD, of the Psychology Department of The Citadel, for their careful review of two drafts of the manuscript and for their many helpful comments and suggestions. Also, thanks must be given to the board of managers of the University Christian Movement in Cleveland for their strong support for the entire Grown-Up Abused Children Program. Additionally, the late Robert Clarke, the previous director of the UCM, must be acknowledged not only for his support and encouragement but for the insight he provided from his own experience of leading a group. We would also like to thank Melissa Leehan and Paul Webb, as well as our children. We sincerely appreciate the patience, support, and forbearance they provided that allowed the time and schedule adjustments necessary for us to complete this new edition.

Of course, none of this would have been possible were it not for the former abuse victims who have participated in the groups. They overcame the paralyzing guilt and fear that had been instilled in them, revealed their experiences, and shared their struggles. Some even offered suggestions about the contents of this book. Without their courage and strong instinct for survival, none of this would have been possible. Thank you all.

Effects of Child Abuse for Adult Survivors

"I came to group because I wanted to learn how to talk to people about myself, I guess, to learn how to trust them."

—Dan, 20-year-old student, survivor of physical abuse

"People always say I look angry, but I don't feel angry. Actually, I don't ever feel much of anything."

—Sarah, 25-year-old secretary, incest survivor

"I thought maybe in a group I could learn how to make friends, but I'm still afraid no one will like me—there's not much to like, I mean, I don't seem to know how to be with people."

—Rich, 23-year-old college senior, survivor of physical abuse, still living with parents who are verbally abusive

Who is a survivor of abuse? Did any of us grow up in a totally nonviolent setting? Probably not. Domestic violence is common in our society. In the introduction to his recent book, John Briere (1992) writes, "The majority of adults raised in North America, regardless of gender, age, race, ethnicity, or social class, probably experienced some level of maltreatment as children" (p. xvii). But what "level of maltreatment" constitutes trauma? or leads to lasting negative effects? or requires legal or therapeutic intervention?

Our purpose in this book is twofold: (a) to promote understanding of the effects of chronic physical, sexual, and psychological child abuse and neglect that occur within the family system; and (b) to illustrate how these effects can be treated through group therapy. Before we consider the long-term effects of abuse and potential treatment strategies, we will define more clearly what we mean by chronic physical, sexual, and psychological child abuse and neglect.

We would like to make three general observations about abuse within family systems before defining specifics. First, we focus on family abuse because we believe it has unique effects on the victims. If one is mugged on a city street, one may justifiably be fearful (at least, for a time) of returning to that same area and may be mistrustful of strangers on the street. If the abuse is inflicted by someone whom the individual knows, a friend, colleague, date, or trusted authority, the mistrust extends not only to the offender, but to one's own judgment and ability to choose friends. If similar forms of abuse occur within one's family, the bruises may be no more painful but their emotional implications are more devastating. "If I am not safe in my own family, where am I safe? Who can I trust?"

Second, family abuse is not always the product of malicious intent. It may be, as we will see, the result of a spanking "getting out of hand" or a parent being physically or emotionally incapable (because of illness, depression, or external constraint) of providing for the care and safety of a child, despite the parent's best intentions. If such incidents occur frequently or create a chronic condition, the resulting emotions for the child of fear, mistrust, or abandonment may be the same as if the abuse had been intentional.

Third, although all forms of abuse are harmful, it is important to acknowledge that there are differential effects. Each form creates different personality and behavioral dynamics. Each may have different effects on later life and different impacts on the physical and emotional development of the child experiencing them (Briere, 1992; McCann & Pearlman, 1990; Smetana, Kelly, & Twentyman, 1984; Wolfe, 1987). The relationship of the abuser to the victim can also affect the long-range impact of the violence. The age of the victim will determine the effects on a child's development. The forms of assistance and support available to the child will influence the range, intensity, and longevity of the effects (Jehu, 1988). All of these factors cannot be examined in detail here, but practitioners should be aware of the many variables that affect their clients and are encouraged to read the above-mentioned sources for greater clarification.

❑ The Many Forms of Abuse

Our definitions are intended to be brief and consistent with the prevailing literature. In general, a behavior should be consid- *Def.* ered abusive when it is harmful to the physical or emotional well-being or psychological development of a child. We will consider the commonly identified forms of child maltreatment: physical, sexual, and psychological abuse and neglect. As we will indicate, these forms are not entirely distinct but the differentiation is helpful for discussion.

PHYSICAL ABUSE

Defining physical abuse can be problematic in American society, where a certain level of physical violence against children is generally considered acceptable, and even necessary, all in the name of effective discipline. As a working definition, we submit that physical abuse involves any behavior of parents or caregivers that harms, or threatens to cause harm, to the physical well-being of a child. It can range from a spanking that gets out of hand to a beating that bruises, breaks bones, or endangers life. More specifically, physical abuse includes, but is not limited to, hitting, kicking, shaking, throwing, squeezing, burning or freezing, and starving or force-feeding a child.

Physical abuse may be the easiest form of child abuse to identify. Bruises, burns, and broken bones are verifiable. Emergency room personnel have learned to distinguish most deliberately inflicted wounds from accidental ones. However, not all physical abuse results in visits to emergency rooms, and bones do not have to be broken for physical abuse to have occurred. Many children are slapped, punched, and even thrown across the room without sustaining injuries requiring medical treatment. Nevertheless, they are harmed, and their physical well-being is threatened.

Furthermore, it also must be acknowledged that when children are physically abused, their sense of security is threatened, not only at the moment of the abuse but for their immediate future. Even if children are too young to articulate them, questions arise: "What did I do to deserve this? When will it happen again? What must I do to avoid more of this?"

We need only reflect on Abraham Maslow's hierarchy of needs to realize the profound impact of such treatment. When children are abused, their physiological needs for safety are not being met. Maslow (1987) maintains that satisfactory fulfillment of this need is essential if a person is to move on to address needs for security and belonging and to develop other aspects of personality. When children live in constant fear for their safety, little attention or energy can be directed to the pursuit of higher goals of love, belonging, and self-esteem. Thus, physical abuse, in addition to harming the body, undermines personality development. We will examine this further when we consider psychological abuse.

SEXUAL ABUSE

Sexual abuse has been defined as "sexual contact, ranging from fondling to intercourse, between a child in mid-adolescence or younger and a person at least five years older" (Briere, 1992, p. 4). The offender may be a parent, but it may also be a stepparent, aunt, uncle, grandparent, older sibling, babysitter, or trusted neighbor. He or she may be of the same or different sex as the child. Sexual abuse may also include visual exposure and verbal innuendo of a sexual nature. The critical issues are that (a) the sexual contact is initiated and controlled by someone responsible for the care, protection, and well-being of the child; and (b) such contact is considered socially inappropriate because of disproportion of power, age difference, or family relationship.

The sexual contact may or may not involve physical violence. If the sexual act is accompanied by force, the child experiences the dual abuse of physical pain and sexual exploitation. The child is physically attacked, intimately violated, and emotionally traumatized.

Most often, the trusted authority figure does not force the child into sexual activity. Rather, he cajoles, tricks, or manipulates the child into a sexual relationship. The child may be convinced that such contact is okay. It is "what you do to be nice to your uncle." Or it is "something I must do" to be treated well.

But another message is soon added. "This is something just between us. This is our little secret." The act that was supposedly good is now wrong, even though the child may not be able to explain why. It is often at this point that the threat of violence to the child or others is added. "If you tell anyone, I will hurt you or your sister or . . ."

Thus, sexual abuse, like physical abuse, has psychological and emotional components. Not only does sexual abuse destroy the caring and protective relationship between child and caregiver, but it also undermines the child's sense of safety within the family. The wall of secrecy created by the perpetrator cuts the child off from other sources of support. Even while living walled off by secrecy, the victim cannot help but wonder, if only subconsciously, why other members of the family do not interfere. The child internalizes negative messages of not being valued within the total family system, or may distort the reality of who is "in charge" or "at fault" and become convinced of his or her own "badness" (Courtois, 1988; Summit, 1983).

PSYCHOLOGICAL ABUSE

As noted above, all abuse has psychological dimensions (McCann & Pearlman, 1990; Navarre, 1987). Physical beatings damage a child's body but also undermine his or her sense of safety and trust of caregivers. Sexual abuse damages a child's self-image and sense of value. These are just a few of the effects; further discussion follows in later chapters. Such effects are often the most devastating and long-lasting aspects of the abuse experience, as well as the most difficult to identify and treat. As David Wolfe (1987) points out, "The psychological nature of maltreatment . . . is more difficult to record and is suspected to be more damaging to the child than physical injuries" (p. 18).

The definition of psychological abuse that we present below is adapted from the findings of the International Conference on Psychological Abuse of Children and Youth (see Garbarino, Guttman, & Seeley, 1986, and Hart, Germain, & Brassard, 1987) and includes an eighth item added by Briere (1992). Eight types of parent or caretaker behaviors are included in this definition: (a) rejecting (e.g., avoiding or pushing the child away); (b) degrading/devaluing (e.g., criticizing or humiliating the child); (c) terrorizing (e.g., physically or psychologically threatening, or verbally assaulting the child); (d) isolating (e.g., depriving the child of social contact or interaction); (e) corrupting (e.g., teaching antisocial behaviors); (f) exploiting (e.g., using the child to meet parental needs); (g) denying essential stimulation, emotional responsiveness, or availability (e.g., lack of loving caregiving); and (h) unreliable and inconsistent parenting (e.g., inconsistent support, contradictory demands, etc.) (see also Garbarino & Gilliam, 1980; Garbarino et al., 1986; Hart et al., 1987).

Psychological abuse is difficult to measure or document. The childhood retort, "Sticks and stones may break my bones, but words will never hurt me," is not true if the words come repeatedly from the lips of mothers and fathers, those people who supposedly know and love you best. Then, the words can hurt forever.

Such abuse even may be inflicted without words; it can be done by exploiting a child's vulnerability. Children are by nature dependent. To survive and thrive, they need regular care, nurturance, and emotional support, as well as adequate food, clothing, and shelter. Their characters and personalities, as well as their minds and bodies, are in the process of formation. They are highly susceptible to forces around them. They know they are dependent and have few, if any, resources outside of their families upon which to draw. So when a child is paraded naked before snickering visitors, not allowed to play with other children, locked in a closet for long periods of time, forced to watch pets or property being destroyed, or threatened with being given or sold to an unsavory relative or neighbor, the child has little or no choice but to submit to the ridicule and intimidation. Such a child learns to live in constant dread and to accept such conditions as a "normal" way of life. Although no blow may ever be struck, such children live in fear that they may be the next victim of the same violence that destroyed their beloved pet. Even though no specific insult is uttered, their personal development is severely hampered by that fear.

Sometimes, such intimidation is experienced when children watch one parent beat the other. They wonder, "Is this fighting my fault? What did I do wrong? Will I be the next object of this anger? (Often, they are.) What will happen to me if they separate? What will become of me if he kills her?" Children experience a profound lack of control over their family life.

Such thoughts and feelings may or may not be the result of specific remarks by either parent, but the emotional distress is nevertheless real. The pain and fear of the moment are no less intense and the psychological wounds no less deep. The negative, frightening messages embedded in the minds and hearts of the children can be as deep as if they had been driven there by blows. Those messages can taint their view of themselves and other people even into adulthood. The violence they observe between their parents colors their view of marriage relationships and teaches them violent methods of conflict resolution.

NEGLECT

The forms of abuse we have discussed thus far are all active, no matter how subtly they may be expressed. They involve the utterance of a word or the commission of a deed that hurts a child. Neglect, on the other hand, is indirect. The abuse is not inflicted by words or deeds but rather by words not spoken and deeds not performed—acts of omission.

A child's physical welfare is threatened because food, clothing, shelter, health care, and hygiene are not provided. This is the most common form of abuse investigated by child protection services. A child also can be emotionally starved because caring words are never spoken and signs of affection are never offered. Neglect is the failure of caregivers either to provide for the physical and medical needs of children under their care or to meet a child's emotional, affectionate, or support needs.

Physical neglect is often discovered when children are brought to emergency rooms because they are suffering from malnutrition or diseases resulting from unsanitary living conditions. A child also may be suffering from simple childhood diseases that have been allowed to progress to dangerous levels. Neglect also may be identified when a neighbor reports that a young child is being left alone for long periods of time, or that children are being left to fend for themselves at an age when they do not have the capacity to care for themselves or protect themselves from harm. School personnel sometimes discover neglect when repeated school absences are investigated.

Emotional neglect occurs when parents fail to provide adequate affection and nurturance for their children. Emotional neglect is difficult to identify. One way it has been discovered in medical settings is when an infant is brought in who is failing to grow and develop even though adequate food is available. Such a medical condition, sometimes called nonorganic "failure to thrive" (there are also organic causes for this condition), stems from the fact that the child has not received adequate human contact (Kempe & Helfer, 1980). The child is fed adequate food, but has not been held, hugged, or cuddled enough to fulfill its emotional needs. The child's body fails to metabolize its food because it is starved for human affection. No matter how much food is available, the child is too emotionally and physically listless to take advantage of it. A very effective medical treatment for such children is simply that they be held and hugged while being fed.

Most emotional neglect does not have dramatic physical effects. Neglected children learn to adapt to a lack of physical contact. They come to expect that their mother will not touch them, will seldom speak to them, and will ignore them for long periods of time. Such children may accommodate this lack of nurturing by becoming sullen, withdrawn, and even hostile as they learn that the world is a cold, lonely, and unfriendly place. Emotional neglect often stems from the parents' inability to provide for their own needs, let alone those of a child. The parent may be sick, alcoholic or chemically dependent, depressed, and unable to function in a caring or supportive way. In such a family, the children are forced to take care of themselves in ways far beyond the skills appropriate to their age. A 5-year-old cares for younger siblings. A 7-year-old cooks for a family of six. A teenager is responsible for filling out Aid to Families With Dependent Children forms and negotiating with welfare agencies for family support. Even as they perform their tasks well, such responsibilities strain the psychological capacities of these children.

In such families, the children are taking over the roles of their parents. They are fulfilling many of the caregiver roles that are more appropriately the parents' responsibilities. Often, the roles that the children perform are not merely those of physical caregiver; they also become responsible for the emotional care and nurturing of the parents. Because Mother is "feeling poorly," they must soothe and comfort her. Because Daddy is often drunk, he cannot be a supportive partner to his wife, so the child must fulfill that role. In such families, the children's needs are seldom met. They are left emotionally starved.

We have offered some definitions and brief descriptions of various forms of child abuse and neglect. The immediate effects of child abuse and neglect are sometimes observed, and intervention is provided. For many victims, however, it is not until much later in life that intervention is sought or offered when the long-term effects become apparent. The remainder of this chapter is devoted to the long-term effects of child abuse and neglect.

❏ Long-Term Effects of Child Abuse and Neglect

Over the course of our work with adult survivors of abuse and neglect, we have repeatedly heard appeals for help in learning how to trust others, how to take control over chaotic lives, how to deal with feelings, and how to "feel better about myself." These "presenting problems" often profoundly hinder or prevent these adults from functioning as happy, healthy, and productive individuals.

We believe that most of these problems are, in fact, the long-term effects of childhood experiences that were marked by frequent, repetitive psychological, physical, or sexual abuse or neglect. Many of these long-term effects of child abuse have been noted by other researchers and clinicians (Briere, 1992; Browne & Finkelhor, 1986; Courtois, 1988; Helfer, 1978; McCann & Pearlman, 1990; McCann, Pearlman, Sakheim, & Abrahamson, 1988).

Our conceptualization of how and why these problems develop takes into account the cognitive, affective, and behavioral effects of abuse as well as the interpersonal dynamics of the abusive family. The model put forth by McCann et al. (1988) to explain the long-term effects of childhood sexual abuse clearly states our position:

> The basic tenet of the model is that the individuals hold certain beliefs and expectations (schemata) about the self and others, which both shape and are shaped by their experience in the world. Various feelings are attached to these beliefs. The main implication of this notion for understanding childhood sexual abuse victims is that a victim's unique interpretation of the trauma determines his or her reactions (emotional, cognitive, and behavioral) to that trauma, which in turn affect his or her subsequent interactions with others. (p. 78)

Thus, we can expect that children growing up in a dysfunctional family where abuse is an almost daily experience will acquire distorted beliefs about themselves and others. These distorted beliefs may well foster emotional responses that are inappropriate or maladaptive and result in coping behaviors that are ineffective or undesirable.

PROBLEM AREAS RESULTING FROM ABUSE AND NEGLECT

We have identified five areas where abuse survivors encounter difficulties in functioning. These will dictate the goals for groups to be discussed in the next chapter. Briefly, these problem areas are:

1. A basic lack of trust in oneself and others that interferes with, and sometimes even precludes, one's ability to establish meaningful and intimate interpersonal and sexual relationships

2. Deeply ingrained feelings of low self-esteem that are often reflected in disparaging self-statements and the belief that "no one could possibly care about me because I'm not worth it"

3. A sense of powerlessness and lack of control that frequently results in an inability to make decisions and that is manifested by many adult survivors in haphazard, seemingly unplanned life goals and events

4. Difficulty in identifying, acknowledging, and disclosing feelings, especially evident in the underlying, frequently debilitating, unresolved feelings of anger, guilt, and depression

5. Lack of expertise in basic social skills, which further impedes the ability to establish friendships and other relationships

Of course, not all adult survivors of childhood abuse struggle with all of these problems, but the problems occur frequently enough in greater or lesser degree to be noteworthy. We also will consider briefly some of the lasting effects specific to sexual abuse.

❏ Lack of Trust

One virtually universal problem identified by researchers (Finkelhor, 1988; Helfer, 1978; Leehan & Wilson, 1985; McCann & Pearlman, 1990; McCann et al., 1988) and adult survivors themselves is the great difficulty the survivors have in learning to trust themselves and others. We believe that this inability to trust is the basis for many of the other problems these adults face.

Developmentally, establishing trust is one of the first requirements for healthy personality formation. Indeed, according to Erikson's (1963) theory of human development, the first psychosocial developmental crisis all humans encounter is trust versus mistrust. This stage begins at birth and continues as a major focus into early childhood. The developmental task of this stage is for the infant/child to learn to trust the primary caregivers, and from this experience to trust oneself and others. This sense of trust implies that "one has learned to rely on the sameness and continuity of the outer providers, but also that one may trust oneself . . . and one is trustworthy" (p. 248).

LEARNING NOT TO TRUST OTHERS

For trust to develop effectively, children need parents who are consistent in their nurturing and other caretaking behaviors. Consistency in nurturing enables children to learn that they are valued and safe. Consistency in behavioral response allows children to determine that certain behaviors will elicit predictable, consistent responses.

Appropriate responses also are necessary if children are to learn to trust their caregivers and others. Parents who take advantage of a child's affection and vulnerability for their own gratification (sexual or emotional) distort a child's needs and disrupt the child's ability to believe that his or her needs truly can be met. Abusive parents frequently are not predictable or consistent in their behavior, reactions, and attitudes toward their children, or they take advantage of a child's openness and vulnerability. Behaviors that receive laughter and applause on one day may be met with verbal or physical punishment on another day. Expressions of affection become experiences of discomfort and disgust. These varied and unpredictable responses have two negative effects. First, they teach the children not to trust their parents; instead, they learn to be guarded and to expect betrayal and disappointment. These children frequently become excessively cautious and watchful, characteristics that often continue into adulthood. This mistrust also may be generalized to others in the world because the children do not learn to believe that others are trustworthy.

LEARNING NOT TO TRUST ONESELF

More critical, however, is the fact that abused children learn not to trust themselves because they often cannot distinguish which behaviors will elicit the desired responses from their parents. As adults, they may act tentatively, testing carefully for responses from others, providing caveats and qualifications before committing to an opinion or action, afraid of what the response will be.

In addition, when these adults do reach the point of wanting to trust someone, the fear of betrayal and the need to "test" the person frequently interfere with the process of learning to trust. The testing may take a variety of forms, but the end message is always the same: "Prove that you still love me by tolerating one more unfair demand or passing one more test." Needless to say, this testing is self-defeating and at times results in the loss of a friend or loved one, thus confirming what the adult believed from the beginning—that he or she is not worthy or deserving of being loved.

The following example will illustrate more graphically how the process of learning to trust is an ongoing struggle to change one's beliefs about the safety and trustworthiness of others.

> Marie was a 23-year-old college honor student, outstandingly bright, but equally insecure and afraid to trust or be close to people. She lived with her father and stepmother, an uneasy arrangement because her father, although no longer physically abusive, continued to harass and criticize her verbally and emotionally. She had lost her mother during her adolescence through an apparent suicide. By the time she joined the group in her early 20s, Marie had perfected a system of communicating that kept her safely distant from, although apparently related to, other people. In daily life, she had several friends who knew little or nothing about her abusive history and who found her to be a witty, charming, and at times brilliant conversationalist, as well as a steadfast, loyal friend. Within the group where self-disclosure was a prerequisite for healing, she barely spoke a word and appeared frightened and withdrawn, although obviously attentive.
>
> Finally, during the second year, the female leader was able to break through the isolation and loneliness and began to draw Marie out. The cause of the initial breakthrough remains an enigma. It appears that the female leader and Marie shared some unspoken common bond for one another, perhaps a basic understanding of the intense need that Marie had to be loved and cared for. At any rate, the long, slow process of learning to open up and trust was begun.
>
> Frequently, it was a "one step forward, three steps backward" procedure. One week, Marie would feel safe and begin to disclose her past and her needs. The following three meetings, she would be unable to utter a word for fear of being hurt or punished for sharing. As the female leader and other group members continued to offer support and reassurance over time, Marie's need to retreat back into herself diminished.
>
> What happened next showed her increased strength and trust as well as her continuing insecurity and need for reassurance. She began to test the female leader. She would call her at home at times when she knew it would be difficult for the leader to talk with her and provide support. She would make greater demands on the leader's

time outside the group, waiting to see if the leader would reject her. Through it all, she would also remain self-effacing and passive-aggressive, laying out the demands and fearfully waiting to see if the leader would provide reassurance one more time.

Interestingly, as the relationship between the two continued to develop, the demands peaked and the testing became more intermittent. A turning point was reached when the leader finally confronted Marie with the impossibility of meeting all her needs. The leader expressed her own frustration at not being able to "do it all" because she was also a fallible human being. This revelation to Marie seemed to change the nature of the relationship, enabling Marie to see the leader as more "human" and to attain a fuller understanding of the nature of human relationships.

TRUST AND REJECTION

For many adult survivors, the fear of rejection results in protective behaviors that are in direct opposition to the desire for support and reassurance from others. They may struggle with conflicting needs. In part, they want to reach out and connect with others so that they may receive the support they need, but the fear of being rejected holds them back in silent longing, protected but alone.

As they are able to become more aware of these conflicting needs and realize when they are testing or making unfair demands on others, they can begin to take greater control of their own behavior. They can learn more direct ways of asking people for what they need and realize that another's inability to always meet their needs is a human failing and not a sign of rejection. This insight can free them and allow them to begin to trust others.

SAFETY AS AN EXTENSION OF TRUST

Another component of the trust issue is maintaining safety. McCann et al. (1988) view safety as a separate dimension apart from trust and define it as self-safety, or "one's belief in the ability to protect oneself from harm, injury, or loss" (p. 81), and other-safety, or the ability to protect oneself from harmful others.

We see the safety issue as an extension of trust. If people cannot protect themselves or behave in such a way that others do not attack them, they learn not to trust themselves or their ability to interact appropriately or safely with others. On the other hand, the more they learn to trust themselves—their own perceptions, reactions, and judgments—the more confident they feel and the more assertive they become in relation to others. This increase in confidence and assertiveness enables them to act in a more self-protective manner and allows them to begin to feel safer with others.

❏ Low Self-Esteem

Feelings of low self-esteem seem to arise out of the inability to trust oneself and others. According to Erikson (1963), the ability to trust oneself and others "forms a basis in the child for a sense of identity which will later combine a sense of being 'all right,' of being oneself, and of becoming what other people trust one will become" (p. 248). We have found that abused children typically do not believe that they are "all right."

NEGATIVE MESSAGES

In fact, the contrary message is more often heard and believed, resulting in a distorted system of beliefs about themselves and others. Abusive parents frequently tell their children that they are not all right, that they are stupid or ugly or unlovable, and that they are incapable of achieving or being successful. Even if critical words are not used, attitudes, facial expressions, and other actions that show disgust, disdain, or indifference have the same negative effect as do spoken statements.

Children internalize these verbal and nonverbal messages and feel ashamed and unworthy, not good enough to be cared about or valued. They learn to believe that there is something inherently wrong with them, for why else would their parents continually reject, punish, and verbally confirm their lack of worth? In brief, "If your own mother (or father) doesn't like you, who will?" And the conclusion that follows is, "Therefore, there must be something wrong with me." In our groups, we have found that even as adults, these individuals often express feelings of not being "all right," of being unworthy of friends or caring responses from others.

THE EFFECTS OF UNREALISTIC EXPECTATIONS

Another source of negative messages are the unrealistic or impossible expectations that abusive parents have for their children. For example, in many instances, abusive parents act like children themselves and expect their children to take care of them. This type of role reversal is obviously unfair, and even the brightest, most capable children are unable to meet the demands that are placed upon them, or else they do so with great anxiety. Thus, they meet with parental criticism and derision as well as physical abuse.

These children do not realize that what is expected is really too much; instead, they internalize the feelings of anxiety, incompetence, unworthiness, and "badness." Clearly, in reality, the problem lies in the parents' inability to affirm their children as worthwhile human beings and to differentiate between the children as people and the children's behavior.

Sadly, as these children grow up, these feelings of "badness" and unworthiness can interfere with their adult relationships. Several times, group members have talked about the fear and anxiety associated with believing that others might sincerely like or care about them, a phenomenon that one person has called "waiting for the other shoe to drop." This fear manifests itself in the belief that "if people say they like me or are kind to me, I know that sooner or later something bad will happen; they will hurt me in some way." That occurrence of something "bad" has been the only consistency in their lives. Sometimes, the pressure of waiting for the "bad" to come is so great that they will actually behave in some self-defeating way or manipulate the situation to bring about a negative consequence, just to relieve the tension.

At one group meeting, we reviewed the progress that members were making toward achieving their goals. One of Jeff's goals was to overcome his extreme shyness and talk more, both at the group meeting and in other settings. He had made substantial progress on this goal in the group setting, and he no longer needed to be cajoled, prodded, or pleaded with before voicing an opinion. Members were very positive and enthusiastic about the gains he had made. One could see by the expression on his face that he truly enjoyed all the attention and praise he was receiving. He seemed to glow with happiness.

At the next few meetings, his behavior began to change. He was tense and irritable, and he became more and more silent. He finally regressed to a point where his behavior was similar to what it had been when he first joined the group. Members and group leaders alike were mystified, as well as frustrated, by the change.

After much discussion, it finally became clear that Jeff, at least unconsciously, was reverting back to his old way of behaving. After receiving all the positive reinforcement at the meeting weeks before, he had become nervous and afraid, waiting for the rejection, pain, and hurt that always followed whenever he felt good about something.

Fortunately, members could understand and empathize with his feelings and offered support and reassurance. In time, his behavior changed again, this time in a positive direction, and he regained his self-confidence.

This example illustrates several of the points discussed above: the fears and beliefs survivors have acquired about "bad" always following "good," the feelings of not being truly lovable, and the belief that they are not "all right" and do not deserve love and caring from others. When they experience "good" following "good" on a consistent basis, they can begin to overcome these fears and beliefs and will not have to "make bad things happen" each time they have a positive experience.

SELF-DEFEATING BEHAVIORS

The tendency toward self-defeating behavior also occurs in other areas of the survivor's life, such as failure to complete projects, a chronic "dropping in and out" of college classes, or lack of follow-through in job search or on work-related projects. It has been our experience, when working with adult survivor groups composed primarily of college students, that anxiety levels and fear of failure related to college coursework often become debilitating. Even in cases of extremely bright students who have records of high achievement, the fear of failure and the high anxiety sometimes win out, and the student either drops the course or does poorly on tests and assignments even when well prepared. This almost seems to be an unconscious confirmation of one's inferiority and inability to do well, which becomes a self-fulfilling prophecy. Even repeated successes do not easily erase the learned belief in one's inadequacy.

LACK OF ENTITLEMENT AND
BELIEF IN ONE'S ABILITIES

Another consequence of these feelings of inadequacy is the inability to ask for anything for oneself. This generally comes from the belief that one is not worthy of receiving love, attention, rewards, or anything positive. This belief is compounded by the fact that when something positive happens (for example, when a "reward" is earned and received or attention is given), the initial reaction is of guilt ("I don't deserve this"), followed by a devaluing or discounting of one's own actions ("The test was really easy" or "Anyone could do this").

Sometimes, this inability to advocate for one's own needs stems from the fact that survivors had to focus so intently on the needs of their parents. This was their role in the family. To protect themselves, they had to meet the needs of their parents before those unmet needs became the source of abuse. This often meant that they did not pay attention to their own needs. As a result, they do not recognize their own needs. They do not think their needs are worthy of attention, and even when they can recognize them, these adults often do not know how to ask to have them met.

In addition, we have observed repeatedly that these adults have great difficulty taking any credit for achievements or for having caused something good to happen. Again, this reaction seems to stem directly from childhood experiences in which they were punished or put down when they succeeded, another example of the "other shoe" syndrome. When they did succeed, they were accused of being selfish or prideful or arrogant if they expressed any joy or satisfaction at an achievement.

As adults, they are so certain that they cannot have an effect on the world that when they do, they attribute the result to external circumstances or other people, or else they belittle their own efforts. They make comments such as "I was lucky" or "It was really easy."

One group member went so far as to attribute his success on a test to the fact that it had snowed that day. Obviously, there was no logical connection between his achievement and the weather, but he simply could not take credit for himself or his ability.

Furthermore, these adults have a difficult time listening to and believing praise for their own actions or abilities. Perhaps this is because they never received much praise or other positive reinforcement for their efforts. Interestingly, they feel free to give praise to others but are noticeably uncomfortable when they are on the receiving end.

GRANDIOSITY AS A COMPENSATING BEHAVIOR

Still another, quite different reaction we have noted in some individuals is a kind of exaggerated statement of competence, or self-aggrandizement. These adults may make grandiose statements about their talents or intelligence. Even though these statements are objectively accurate, they have not been able to use their talents and intelligence to achieve any productive outcomes. In fact, many of these adults are quite bright and talented, and they are angry and bitter that their lives have not been such that their gifts were nurtured and developed. This bitterness contributes to immobility, which further inhibits the development of their talents. Although this anger is often quite understandable, it becomes dysfunctional when used as an excuse for continued lack of action, productivity, or goal setting. Their boastful statements—without concrete evidence of achievement—often alienate or intimidate others, resulting in increased feelings of isolation and loneliness. Several examples of this low self-esteem coupled with self-defeating behavior readily come to mind.

> One is the case of Jerry, a 36-year-old man, who has been employed only occasionally. He still lives with his parents, who continue to be disparaging of his abilities and neglectful of his needs. Although exceptionally intelligent, especially in mathematics, repeated attempts at college all ended in only partial success or failure. Jerry alternates between considering himself a failure and striking out at a world that is insensitive to his needs and his gifts. He vehemently asserts to all who will listen how high his IQ is, and how colleges are

not designed to meet the needs of geniuses. He feels the need for a one-on-one nurturing of his abilities and talents, not the traditional classroom approach of one teacher to 20 or 30 students. Thus, he blames his lack of success on his inability to bend to a system that he considers inhuman.

Jerry received much support as well as hard feedback from group members, and particularly the male group leader, about the self-defeating nature of his behavior. He was encouraged to try things that had a reasonable hope of success and received support, reassurance, and consolation even when the attempts were not successful. Over time, he was able to become assertive in a more positive way instead of criticizing the "system" that he perceived as holding him back.

That there is some fact in Jerry's belief is true; however, there is also the part of him that fears that were he to actually find someone who provided a one-on-one experience, he just might not succeed. Thus, his attempts at reaching out become carefully structured to elicit rejection.

We have attempted to illustrate the three patterns of self-defeating behavior that we have seen adult survivors use in an effort to protect themselves from hurt or disappointment. Each of the patterns stems from the low self-esteem experienced by these adults. The underlying beliefs, fears, and feelings of inadequacy are deeply ingrained, and the behavioral responses are often unconscious. Even in cases where the individual is aware of the behavior, change is difficult to enact.

The intentional "messing up" offers a relief from the tension that builds as they wait for something bad to happen. They believe that bad things will happen to them because they do not deserve anything good. For the same reason, they cannot ask for anything for themselves or take credit for their accomplishments, except in extreme cases where they take too much credit and become grandiose.

❑ Power and Control

This lack of trust in oneself, coupled with belief in one's own inadequacy and incompetence, often leads to what McCann and

Pearlman (1990) call "disturbed power schemas" (p. 164), that is, a sense of powerlessness and helplessness, a feeling of not having control of one's life. The inability to protect themselves is a frequent and very real experience for abuse victims. As previously noted, former victims often attribute both successes and problems to external causes. They frequently do not see the role they play in a given situation (unless it is the role of victim) or the options that are available to them. Survivors of abuse often are unable to perceive themselves as powerful or capable of taking control and making decisions to govern their lives. Some actually choose friends or partners who are controlling or abusive, continuing the cycle of abuse (Helfer, 1978).

If we consider the second stage of development in Eriksonian theory, we can easily discern the roots of these adult feelings of inadequacy, insecurity, and low self-esteem. Erikson believes that children need to learn autonomous, self-defined behavior. This is accomplished as children gain independence and achieve a degree of control over their environment.

To do this, children need opportunities to practice independent activities in a safe environment that does not offer excessive restrictions or unreasonable punishment. This requires self-confident, autonomous role models as well as parents who can help set limits while allowing the children some freedom of choice. In the abusive family, the parents frequently do not have control of their own lives. They are unable to set reasonable limits for themselves, are insecure, and have little self-confidence. They may be rigid and unrealistic in setting rules and standards, and often they are overly punitive when their child fails to live up to expected standards, even when these standards are unfair, irrational, or impossible. Additionally, the parents may be frivolous or inconsistent about the standards they set. This lack of clarity related to standards further removes any possibility of control from the child's life because he or she cannot discern which behaviors or rules are appropriate to various situations. In extreme cases, children are sometimes physically abused because they have not achieved standards that are ambiguous, or subject to frequent change.

LOSS OF CONTROL THROUGH
LOSS OF DECISION-MAKING SKILLS

One way that individuals are able to take control of their lives is by learning effective problem-solving and decision-making skills. Children growing up in an abusive family rarely have the opportunity for such learning. Frequently, abusive parents are out of control of their own lives because they do not know how to solve problems or make decisions. They cannot serve as good role models for decision making. Furthermore, they often place their children in situations that preclude the learning of effective decision making.

NO GUIDANCE FOR MAKING CHOICES

For example, children may be asked to make decisions without the benefit of proper guidance or information for generating and analyzing possible alternatives. Thus, the children never learn that there can be an effective process for making decisions. A haphazard choosing of whatever is easy, available, or readily apparent as a course of action often follows. The chances for success using this type of problem-solving strategy are drastically minimized.

NO OPPORTUNITY TO MAKE A CHOICE

Another scenario is one in which parents take the decision-making power away from their children. They make decisions for the children without allowing any input into the process. The decision is reported and the children are expected to carry it out. Rarely, if ever, is consideration given as to whether or not the required behaviors for implementation of the decision are appropriate to the children's developmental level or realistic in terms of their skills and abilities. Again, the likelihood of a successful outcome is diminished. Instead, these children are set up for failure, blame, and shame.

NO SUCCESS IN MAKING A CHOICE

Still another example is perhaps the most confusing and destructive. In this case, the parents continually change their expectations or standards so that the children learn that behaviors chosen and acted out one day are not effective or applicable the next day. This leads these children to believe that the choices they make and the actions they perform do not really make a difference.

No matter what choice they make and no matter how well they execute it, it is never good enough. They are still subject to being ignored, ridiculed, or beaten. Over and over again, group members recount tales of how their decisions were ridiculed and their accomplishments were turned into reasons for abuse. The achievement was "pure luck." They were "too arrogant" about their success. It was "done for the wrong motives." The end result is that they never learned that it is possible for them to make a correct choice or accomplish anything worthwhile. In fact, the inverse is true. They can never do anything right; they will never amount to anything.

LEARNED HELPLESSNESS

All three of these scenarios promote feelings of helplessness and inadequacy in children and reaffirm their beliefs that they can have no effect on their environment. Social learning theorists have studied the development of learned helplessness in children and adults. Seligman (1975) aptly describes what seems to occur in the case of abused children. These children learn that certain outcomes (e.g., abuse, neglect, violence) and responses (their behaviors) are independent occurrences. If these children believe that others can control outcomes by behaving in certain ways but that they cannot (either because they lack the skills or do not know the effective behaviors), they learn to feel personally helpless.

Over time, as these children repeatedly experience an inability to control or affect outcomes through their own behaviors, they may generalize their beliefs about their helplessness to other situations.

This generalization also results in lowered self-esteem because these children believe that others, who are perceived as more competent, are "better" than they believe themselves to be.

These distorted beliefs about their own personal power, and the helpless behaviors that abused children have learned, complicate and interfere with their ability to learn effective decision-making skills. These children begin with an underlying belief in their own inadequacy or incompetence in affecting their own life circumstances. Add to this a lack of parental role models to demonstrate how to make choices or how to set reasonable guidelines or expectations, and one finds abused children growing up unable to identify with or effectively act upon alternatives for making decisions or solving problems.

In addition, the nonsupportive environment of the abusive family greatly limits opportunities for learning and practicing problem-solving and decision-making skills. That is, abused children tend not to receive encouragement for making decisions, and when they occasionally do make a choice, parental response is inconsistent and often punitive, regardless of the rationality and appropriateness of the decision.

Thus, decision making becomes an impossible ordeal because one cannot see alternatives and "read the cues" ahead of time to anticipate the probable reactions of others to the decisions. Often, the choice is to make no decision and to simply "let things happen." Thus, the opportunity for feeling any sense of ownership or responsibility for the outcomes is lost, and the feeling of helplessness and loss of control over one's life increases.

The following case study illustrates how this lack of control dynamic affected the life of one group member.

Lauretta was a pretty, outwardly vivacious 19-year-old whose father had died when she was about 11 years old. Her mother, a noncommunicative and passive woman, became even more withdrawn after her husband's death. In searching for a meaningful parental relationship, Lauretta turned to a neighbor who served initially as a surrogate father. Over time, he took advantage of her need for closeness and sexually abused her.

Although bright and competent and able to make easy decisions related to her schoolwork, when it came to her social life, she "wandered" in and out of relationships with men as if trying to find an answer to a question she didn't quite understand. At the time she joined the group, she was involved with a young man who was slightly older than herself. She said that she felt positive about this relationship because in the past, she had been drawn to or "chosen" by men who, in her words, "were old enough to be my father." This new relationship seemed to her to be more appropriate and a statement of her growing control over her own love life.

Unfortunately, as time progressed, her new boyfriend seemed to be confused and less certain about the relationship. He told Lauretta that he cared about her, but just didn't think he was ready to be totally committed to one person. Lauretta could understand and acknowledge his confusion. She was even supportive of him. After all, as she stated herself, they were both pretty young.

The issue came to a head when the boyfriend couldn't decide what to do about the relationship and laid the responsibility back on Lauretta. She responded with anger, tears, and frustration and blamed him for not "staying the same," for messing up the relationship with his confusion and honesty.

When group members tried to get her to consider the various alternatives she had for making a decision about the relationship, she refused to listen. She kept repeating, "I don't know what to do. I can't make this or that decision." Her choice was to do nothing, and eventually the boyfriend slowly withdrew from her. She made feeble, covert attempts to stay in touch with him and salvage the relationship by visiting his mother and sister when he wasn't home, but could not make a decision to be either committed to or separate from him.

Although the lack of decision-making skills was part of the problem in the scenario depicted above, the more significant issue revolved around the absence of power and control. Although the group members were willing and able to help this individual learn the necessary skills, she could not break out of her refuge of helplessness that had been learned and reinforced so strongly in her earlier years. Even the loss of a desired relationship was not a strong enough incentive.

COMFORT WITH CHAOS

A sense of powerlessness and helplessness may also create what we call a *comfort with chaos*, the experience that a lack of control and sense of unpredictability is a person's most familiar and comforting condition. They know chaos as a way of life, and anything else is unnatural and disturbing.

Violence within the family of origin contributes to the experience of chaos as a way of life, but this familiarity is also fostered in abusive families in other, more subtle ways. Family roles are frequently ill-defined, inconsistently applied, or totally reversed. Parents fluctuate from being extremely passive, dependent persons needing to be cared for by their children to being overbearing, violent dictators of their household. Parental expectations for their children range from normal household tasks and appropriate childhood behaviors to responsibilities far beyond their young abilities. This inconsistency creates external confusion about one's roles and responsibilities (Courtois, 1988) and internal chaos as the child tries to process the changing demands.

Blair and Rita Justice (1976), in their book *The Abusing Family,* have identified "shifting symbiosis" as a major aspect of the abusing family's interaction process. By this they mean that the process of dependence between and among members of the family is constantly changing and is "not for cooperative mutual support and affection but for exploitation and the satisfaction of neurotic needs" (p. 70). In such a family, it is not just the children who need and seek care and nurturance but the parents as well. There is a constant struggle to determine who will receive more care and have more of their needs satisfied. Thus, the responsibility for providing care shifts among all members of the family.

This struggle goes on without regard for age, maturity, role in the family, or level of ability to provide the care. Very simply, the loser in the battle ends up with the responsibility. Frequently, when the child interferes with a parent's ability to get his or her needs met, or when the child fails to personally meet a parent's need, abuse occurs.

This continual struggle for nurturance and care creates constant change and chaos. Roles within the family are always being readjusted, and reliable support systems are nonexistent. Because of these shifting symbiotic relationships, normal dependency needs are never met, and the family does not fulfill its task as a place where children learn to meet their need to belong yet also learn to become individuals. The constant competition for caring in the abusive family is so dysfunctional that children do not learn to differentiate themselves as individuals. They cannot feel strong and independent or comfortable with themselves. They feel powerless. They do not believe that they can care for themselves, and they believe that to survive, they must find someone who will take care of them.

The search for nurturance moves outside the family. The process of manipulating others to meet one's own needs finds new targets, and what Ray Helfer (1978), in his book *Childhood Comes First*, calls the World of Abnormal Rearing (W.A.R.) Cycle (p. 36) expands into new arenas and inappropriate areas of life such as the workplace, friendships, or new families.

This World of Abnormal Rearing continues to influence other aspects of the victims' lives. Adult survivors carry with them dysfunctional methods for getting their needs met, guilt for not fulfilling unrealistic expectations, and confusion over their roles and responsibilities.

❏ Dealing With Feelings

Dealing with their emotional reactions to their abuse experience is another common problem for survivors. Often, this problem also encroaches on other aspects of a survivor's emotional life. Because many feelings are closely connected (e.g., love and hate, anger and sadness or hurt), and emotions generated by different situations can feel amazingly similar, it is sometimes difficult to distinguish clearly which feelings are being triggered and what is causing the emotional reaction. This can create many problems for survivors.

The overwhelming nature of their abuse experience naturally prompts victims to respond with a wide range of defense mechanisms, from denial, minimization, and dissociation to repression, isolation, and sublimation. It is impossible for us to fully analyze all of these processes in this book; we will discuss those that most directly affect working with survivors in groups. We would refer readers to Nancy McWilliams's (1994) excellent, nonpathologizing treatment of primary and secondary defensive processes in her book

Psychoanalytic Diagnosis (pp. 96-144), and with her remind our readers that

> The person whose behavior manifests defensiveness is generally trying unconsciously to accomplish one or both of the following ends: (1) the avoidance or management of some powerful, threatening feeling, usually anxiety but sometimes . . . other disorganizing emotional experiences; and (2) the maintenance of self-esteem. (p. 97)

These are worthy goals made more difficult for survivors by their abuse. Our work is to help them manage the effect of their trauma in ways that can enhance their lives.

THE UNTENABLE CHOICE: BE OVERWHELMED OR BE NUMB

Feeling overwhelmed is a common experience for victims. When they were being abused, they were frequently overpowered by their attacker, and their feelings of fear, anger, sadness, and so on were overwhelming. To survive, they often withdrew into another state of consciousness, mentally denied what was happening to them, or dissociated from the experience.

These defense processes often worked well for victims during their abuse. However, the processes can be counterproductive when they overflow into other areas of victims' lives. Sometimes, survivors will be reminded of their abusive experience by something that has little or no direct connection, yet they will feel as overwhelmed as they did during the abuse. They again feel out of control. This sense of a lack of control over their feelings and their strong reaction to related occurrences in later life often bring survivors into therapy as they try to understand and sort out the depth of their emotional reaction. Unless they can clearly distinguish their abuse experience from present similar circumstances or learn more productive defense mechanisms (e.g., rationalization or sublimation), their choices seem to be amnesia or emotional devastation.

One solution frequently employed is the denial of the presence of any affect, especially difficult emotions like fear or anger. It is not unusual to observe participants in a group for adult survivors of childhood abuse sitting with tightly controlled body postures, hands and teeth clenched, all muscles tensed, eyes flashing, insisting that they are fine, relaxed, and not at all upset. Often, they are totally unaware of the nonverbal messages that their bodies are sending. Even when these behaviors are pointed out and other people acknowledge that, given similar circumstances, they, too, would be frightened or outraged, some survivors will claim to be totally unmoved and experiencing no emotion at all.

The incongruity between affect and behavior is not limited only to the expression of negative emotions. Feelings of happiness are also denied or repressed. Many former abuse victims report almost no experience of joy, exhilaration, or even satisfaction. What they report is a total shutdown or absence of feeling. Wilson (1980) and Lifton (1979) have identified similar behavior in other victims of traumatic experiences and call it *psychic numbing.*

This reaction is understandable, perhaps even predictable, because the "shutting down" or "numbing" of feelings is not a selective process. In general, it is not possible to shut down only the unpleasant feelings. Most emotions are interrelated and connected. It is commonly recognized that love and hate are frequently interchangeable. Anger often grows out of pain or fear or sadness. Because of these close relationships, survivors know they must repress most feelings in order to control the unacceptable ones.

In addition, these adults often were punished as children for being too exuberant. At best, parents frowned upon and discouraged the excessive activity associated with these children's joy of accomplishment. Even as they grew older and did not express their satisfaction so boisterously, they usually found that achievements were not met with praise or reinforcement but rather became occasions for ridicule or physical beatings designed to "put them in their place." Two lessons were learned: Joy should not be expressed or even felt, and happiness is followed by pain. The ultimate lesson was that it is best not to be happy or to express or acknowledge any emotion at all.

This belief is strengthened further by abuse victims' negative self-concept and low self-esteem. They do not believe that they have a right to feel happy or proud, and certainly not angry. Often, the only emotion they will admit to feeling is guilt, which they believe they deserve to feel.

CONTROLLING ANGER

There are, however, those individuals who are so conscious of their anger and other intense feelings that they become immobilized. Sometimes, they believe that if they were ever to begin to express their deep feelings of anger, resentment, and hatred, they would never be able to stop. They feel the emotion so strongly that they believe the only way to be safe is to totally suppress it, to remain rigidly, adamantly in control.

Several factors are at work in this process. First, much of the anger these people feel is directed toward their abusive or nonprotective parents. They believe that such a negative reaction to the people they are "supposed" to love is inappropriate and wrong. Therefore, guilt moves them to repress the feelings.

Second, their experience of growing up in an abusive home has taught them that anger is destructive and frequently results in violence and physical beatings. Never having observed or been taught nonviolent, productive modes of expressing angry feelings, they are fearful that they may repeat the process of abuse in their own lives. Without effective alternative behaviors, the only recourse they see is to totally deny or repress the emotion. Many of these adults tend to intellectualize their anger. They admit that it is reasonable, justified, and a realistic reaction to what they have experienced, but they feel that no purpose would be served and that much destruction and violence might follow were they to express it. Therefore, the rational solution is to talk above it or around it, but never to get in touch with it or feel it. They intellectually acknowledge it but do not work through it emotionally, so it continues as a powerful unresolved issue. Basically, they detach themselves from it. Unfortunately, such detachment is similar to the "shutting down" strategy and may not be used selectively. In detaching from their anger, they lose touch with many other feelings as well.

Others unconsciously displace their anger onto other people, situations, or things. For example, one woman who participated in peace demonstrations in Washington, DC, in the 1970s suddenly realized as she was shouting antiwar slogans that her fierce anger and frustration were directed toward her abusive parents as much as toward the U.S. government. This insight helped her to finally begin dealing with her unresolved anger at her parents. Although this type of displacement may relieve some of the tension temporarily, it does not resolve the underlying issues or bring permanent satisfaction.

Another dynamic sometimes occurs in relation to this unconscious acting out. On occasions when former victims have struck out in a violent fashion, they report that they were not aware of having any feelings of anger. Whether the violent act was directed at their parents, another person, or just some nearby object, there seemed to be no connection between any present feelings and the action being performed. Their actions and feelings were completely dissociated. In some cases, there were not even any apparent precipitating events; the former victims simply performed the violent act with no reason and no identifiable accompanying affect—a generalized striking out. One extreme example of this kind of aggression is the case of Karen.

Karen was part of a group of radical students on a large university campus during the late 1960s when the burning of buildings as a form of protest was prevalent. She participated in setting fire to an ROTC building on campus. She was arrested, convicted, and actually served time in jail for this action.

Years later, as a participant in our group, Karen recalled the event. While talking about her great anger and resentment toward her parents, she had suddenly remembered the apparently unrelated past event. She talked about how she had felt "driven" during her college years by an intense inner energy that she now could understand as her anger and hostility. She told how, as she helped to light the fire, she felt no emotion. Instead, she said she experienced a distance from the event, almost as if she were two people—one on the outside watching dispassionately as "this person" (herself) performed the aggressive act.

Sometimes, anger and hostility are survivors' responses to anxiety and their sense of abandonment and rejection. Their experience in their families was of frequent punishment, ridicule, and not being accepted. Despite their best attempts to win approval and be liked, they failed to achieve the rewards of love and acceptance, and their anger at this continued into adulthood. Now, rather than confront their anxiety and make further efforts to be accepted and approved, they present an angry, hostile face to the world as a protection against further pain.

GUILT

Often, when these wounded adults get beyond the anger, the resentment, and the fear, what frequently shows up is a constant guilt that is reinforced by their belief in their own worthlessness. Even when they are able to admit to and express anger at the treatment from abusing parents, almost invariably, some guilt follows. As many survivors have explained, this guilt comes from two sources. First, they have been told repeatedly that they are supposed to love their parents, and that they are not allowed to be angry at them. Second, society tells them that parents act in the best interests of their children; thus, if they were mistreated, it must have been their own fault (a message also given by their abusive parents). They must deserve the treatment. Therefore, they have no "right" to be angry.

For some, the belief that they have no right to be angry at their parents is generalized to others. Often, they will express guilt at being angry at other people when they are mistreated, even when the anger is justified. This guilt may manifest itself in self-punishment, self-hate, and self-mutilation. At worst, it is apparent in suicide attempts.

An interesting point to note is that even in the case of those who have grappled with and successfully expressed their anger and firmly believe this expression is justified, a nagging uncertainty, a trace of guilt, frequently remains. For these adults, it remains a lifelong process to refute these distorted cognitive messages. It is as if the belief in their own "badness" is so thoroughly ingrained that no matter how successful they become or how hard they work, the internalized "fact" remains that "if only they had been better, their parents would have loved them." Although the physical beatings have ended, and the ties are broken so that the psychological harassment and verbal disparagement are cut off, these adults often remain victims of the negative messages they have internalized.

Another component of survivors' guilt is an incredible degree of compulsiveness to "do the right thing," an unrealistic desire to be perfect. They seem to believe that if only they could have been perfect, they would have been loved and accepted rather than rejected. Of course, because no one can be perfect, they fall short of the mark and become their own worst critics, reaffirming to themselves that they are unlovable and deserving of rejection.

GRIEF

Finally, as survivors get in touch with the fear and the pain beneath the anger, they become aware of the tremendous amount of grief that they feel. This grief takes many forms—grieving for a childhood that never existed, for loving parents who never were or will be, for opportunities lost, for time wasted, for feelings not felt. High anxiety, fear, and depression may occur in conjunction with the realizations that arise from the grieving process. As a person experiences these painful feelings, the group becomes an especially important place where comfort and affirmation may be received, and the isolation often inherent in depression may be combatted.

DEPRESSION

Depression is a common emotional condition for abuse survivors. The chronic rejection by significant others inherent in family violence makes this psychological reaction quite understandable. The depression may stem from different sources. Most survivors live with a tremendous experience of rejection and loss. They did not feel accepted by their parents, and they are burdened with a sense of loss of "family" as they have heard it described and idealized. This source of depression is almost universal for survivors, but there are variations on this common theme. For some, a sense of guilt also permeates their depression. These are the people who have been told repeatedly how bad and evil they are. A certain moral judgment colors their view of themselves. They believe that they are in some way responsible for anything bad that happens.

For others, their depression is based in their experience of emptiness. They have been told they are worthless, ugly, and defective. Their depression is grounded in shame. These survivors feel they can do nothing right, and that they are not worthy of love.

The fact that children in abusive families are discouraged and sometimes punished for expressing feelings contributes to their depression. The expression of pain or grief is not acceptable, anger is punished, and expecting care and comfort is "selfish." The family atmosphere that discourages emotional expression encourages depressive tendencies (McWilliams, 1994, p. 235).

In the group, survivors are given a setting in which they can express their feelings without being ridiculed, punished, or ignored. They can grieve their loss of "family" and develop new, caring relationships that can provide healing for their guilt and shame. They can be allowed a freedom of expression that can ease their depression. Eventually, out of this grieving process comes healing as these courageous adults learn how to let go of the past and move into the future.

❏ Interpersonal Relationships

The lack of trust and the feelings of low self-worth that characterize adult survivors seem to come together most painfully when these individuals go out into the world and attempt to establish relationships with other people. When children grow old enough to attend school, teachers and classmates become increasingly important. As children start to develop relationships with their peers and other adults, they learn that the interactions with their parents in the home are not necessarily typical or appropriate.

In one way, this is a useful insight that causes the children to learn more positive social behaviors and skills; however, it also dramatizes the abnormality of their home environment and their lack of appropriate relationship skills. Feelings of inadequacy rapidly become feelings of inferiority. As they compare themselves to others, they frequently end up rating themselves as "less than," or even worthless. Recognition of the abnormality of the home situation can result in shame and introversion as these children try to keep others from finding out about the abuse. This secretiveness—coupled with the feelings of low self-esteem, lack of interactive skills, and inability to trust others, greatly limits the children's abilities to develop friendships and effectively resolve the pressing psychosocial crises that revolve around doing things beside and with others (Erikson, 1963).

LACK OF SOCIAL SKILLS

We have observed that the lack of social skills continues into adolescence and adulthood, so that many survivors find themselves unable to share personal information or to acknowledge or disclose their feelings. They are therefore unable to develop the intimacy that forms the basis for close, meaningful relationships with others.

Many survivors did not have the experience of focused, supportive conversations with parents, and intentionally limited their own interactions with other children. They have not learned, or had the opportunity to practice, effective communication skills and interpersonal behaviors with others. Often, they feel inadequate and embarrassed that as adults they still cannot do what seems to come so naturally to others. They also may feel that people do not listen to them or pay attention to them. Even when they try to initiate conversation, they don't receive the type of response they want. They believe it is because they don't know the correct words or behaviors and end up feeling embarrassed, awkward, and clumsy. One male group member exhibited particular difficulty in the area of interpersonal communications.

> Ed was first referred to the group by a concerned faculty member. Although he was an exceptionally bright student, Ed was unable to complete the most basic class work and was extremely unsure of himself in any setting, in or out of the classroom.
>
> When he first began to attend the group, Ed appeared completely frightened, kept his eyes cast down, and avoided contact with others both before and after meeting. Although he attended regularly, he participated only minimally in the group. He would respond "yes" and "no" to questions, but when any question demanded a more extensive response, he would ask to be excused from answering.
>
> The group members were very patient with Ed. They were always willing to let him maintain his silence, and they even made supportive statements, such as that they were pleased that he continued to come, and that they hoped he would soon be able to share further with them. In response to this, Ed would simply nod appreciatively.

If the group leaders attempted to pressure Ed to take a more active role, the other members would come to his rescue, supporting his right to maintain his silence.

This went on for some months; gradually, Ed's responses became a bit more complete, and his answers grew to more than one syllable. The story that slowly emerged revealed severe violence and neglect in his infancy and early childhood that included long hours locked in a dark closet, much ridicule, and brutal beatings. Despite having several older brothers and sisters, he did not learn to speak until he was 4 years old.

The isolation, fear, and lack of opportunity to communicate in his childhood carried over into his school years. Although Ed had a near genius IQ, he was unable to relate to and communicate with his teachers, and he did poorly in school. Nevertheless, working primarily on his own, he had been able to master many complicated aspects of physics and math, even though he was usually too frightened and insecure to share what he knew with his teachers.

After many months of regular attendance and progressively increasing participation in the group, Ed was able to share some of his ideas and mathematical formulas with group members. Most of them confessed complete inability to understand Ed's formulas, but this too proved to be a learning experience for him. He realized that people's failure to understand or to respond with enthusiasm did not mean rejection. Ed continued to attend the group for several months and increased his participation. Still, there were many false starts and many sullen silences. It took much support and cajoling by both the leaders and the group members to keep the communication moving. After a time, Ed began to share his ideas with people outside the group, but he always came back to the group for support. "I am going to talk with Professor _____. Does this sound like a good way to approach it? . . . I need some encouragement."

To this day, Ed continues to need periodic strong doses of encouragement. However, he has overcome much of the fear and distrust that contributed to his continual academic failure.

Even for those survivors who have been able to learn enough social skills to project a fairly extroverted exterior, the lack of trust in themselves and others lies just beneath the surface, and the net result may be a number of superficial, friendly relationships that lack depth and are not satisfying or meaningful. These survivors often have strong needs for intimacy that have grown out of the isolation and alienation that they experienced in childhood. In an attempt to compensate for this lack, they may ask or demand too much from friendships and end up feeling disappointed, rejected, and unloved.

DIFFICULTY IN CHOOSING HEALTHY PEOPLE AS FRIENDS

In addition, many adult survivors have not learned how to identify the type of person who could serve as a friend. Their choices seem to follow two scenarios, depending on whether the fact that their needs were not met in their family takes priority or is subordinate to their need to take care of others.

In the first scenario, the individual will often choose a partner whom he or she believes will fulfill his or her needs. The task of filling a lifetime of needs can become overwhelming for a friend and drive him or her away. If the friend is not driven away, the excessive neediness of the relationship may create a "partnership" with a high potential for exploitation. The survivor does not identify the exploitive nature of the relationship (it may seem "normal" or it may be less than or somewhat different from what he or she experienced in the home), so the abuse takes a new form in a new relationship.

In the second case, the individuals' focus is on taking care of others and not on getting their own needs met. There is no reciprocity in these relationships. No one takes care of them, and that is unsatisfying, but they do not know that things can or should be different, or they do not know how to ask for what they want and need so that their relationships can be more balanced. Thus, they feel frustrated and angry and often act in ways that are detrimental to the ends they seek.

The following case study is a typical example of the frustration and anger that is generated by this ineptness at choosing healthy friends or partners and in establishing balance in a relationship.

At age 27, Melissa was an attractive, assertive, sometimes aggressive, single parent who wanted desperately to make contact and establish close relationships with others. Repeatedly, she would extend herself in a supportive, caring way to potential friends who, at times, returned the support, but who for the most part were so needy themselves that they had nothing to return. When they were not able to give back, Melissa would turn angrily on herself and demand to know what was wrong with her. "Why can't I find and choose people who can accept my friendship and return some to me?" she would ask.

In a way, she had the answer. Underneath the hard shell, Melissa was a sensitive, tender, caring young woman with a deep need to love and nurture. Her own need for the intimacy of caring for another caused her to be drawn to people with an equal need to take. As she continued to give and give and not receive anything in return, she became frustrated and finally angry.

Usually, at that point, she would become so upset that she would confront people with their lack of responsiveness and their failure to give back. Her angry behavior would cause them to act defensively, either by shouting back at her or rejecting her. She was correct in her assessment of their defensive reaction, but what she could not see was that this was not intentional or indicative of her inability to be a friend. It was people's own inability to give to others and their need to take that blocked their response to her.

Over time, with feedback from the group, she was able to realize what she was doing and learned to choose people who not only appreciated her need to give, but also had the potential for returning some caring and support to her. With these people, she was able to learn and practice new social skills that included more clearly communicating her needs, thoughts, and feelings, as well as setting appropriate boundaries and realistic expectations.

Some survivors find themselves in an opposite but equally unhealthy and unsatisfying situation, that of becoming overly dependent on another person. They choose a partner or friend who seems to meet their needs. Although this may work for a time, the survivor often is revictimized in the relationship when the person upon whom they have learned to depend begins to exploit their needs.

As the foregoing examples show, counterproductive and unhealthy ways of viewing oneself and relating to others are learned and reinforced day after day when one grows up in an abusive home. The procedures and mind-sets become deeply ingrained. The process for identifying and changing these accumulated patterns also can be long and complicated. We will discuss these in the next chapter.

Before considering group treatment strategies for survivors, we want to examine two additional aspects of the abuse experience: the differential effects of sexual abuse and the effects of memory repression and dissociation.

❏ Differential Effects for Survivors of Sexual Abuse

In addition to struggling with many of the difficulties identified by those who were physically or psychologically abused, survivors of childhood sexual abuse suffer long-term effects related to their sexual functioning. The issues of trust, self-esteem, power and control, emotional response, and interpersonal intimacy are also manifest in their beliefs, feelings, and behavior related to their sexuality and sexual performance.

More research is available on the effects of sexual abuse than on other forms. It is not our intent to provide an extensive examination of these issues because entire volumes (Briere, 1989, 1992; Courtois, 1988; Dolan, 1991; Maltz, 1991; Maltz & Holman, 1987; McCann & Pearlman, 1990; Sgroi, 1988; Westerlund, 1992; Wyatt & Powell, 1988) have been dedicated to this topic. Rather, we will examine the differential effects of sexual abuse that we believe are relevant to group treatment of survivors.

Group leaders should be aware that the degree to which sexual abuse influences adjustment in adulthood is frequently related to the age at which the abuse was experienced, the duration and frequency of the abuse, the victim's relationship to the offender, the ways in which secrecy was imposed, and the reactions of significant people in the child's world (parents, physicians, police) to disclosure of the abuse (Finkelhor, 1979; Gagnon, 1965; Herman, 1981; Jehu, 1988). Regarding this last factor, Leaman (1980) states, "The parents' reaction is probably the greatest single prognostic indicator of emotional effects of an incident of sexual abuse on a child" (p. 22). Basically, if the parent responds with concern and caring for the child and supports disclosure and discussion of feelings, recovery is faster and lasts longer. This assumes that the instance of abuse is made known to and believed by persons in authority. For those children who are sexually abused by a parent and whose experiences are not made known to or believed by other adults, the prognosis is less positive. Their tendencies to repress, deny, and experience guilt are much greater.

According to Maltz and Holman (1987), the sexual repercussions of incest are manifested in three areas: patterns of sexual behavior (what they call "sexual emergence"); sexual orientation and preference; and sexual arousal, response, and satisfaction. Each of these areas will be discussed briefly.

PATTERNS OF SEXUAL BEHAVIOR

Maltz and Holman (1987) found that "survivors often gravitate toward two extreme sexual lifestyles" (p. 69), choosing either social and sexual withdrawal and isolation from peers, or promiscuous and even self-destructive sexual activity. Jehu (1988) concurs that the women survivors he studied experienced isolation and insecurity as well as discord and a sense of inadequacy in their relationships. This affected not only their relationships with men, even their partners, but also with other women.

Herman (1981) also found evidence of this social isolation and self-exploitive sexual activity in her own study of abuse victims. Her study confirmed our experience with members of our groups. She states:

> The isolation these women felt was compounded by their own difficulty in forming trusting relationships. The legacy of childhood was a feeling of having been profoundly betrayed by both parents. As a result, they came to expect abuse and disappointment in all intimate relationships . . . to be exploited. . . . Given these possibilities, most women opted for exploitation. (pp. 99-100)

Women in our groups have reported acting out this "choice" of exploitation without being aware of what they were doing. These women tended to be flirtatious and almost invited sexual overtures through innuendo and suggestive comments. Often, when these women were queried about their behavior and its motivation, they described a search for male approval, even at the cost of exploitation, rather than a desire for sexual contact. These women also expressed some fear of the sexual experience, but somehow they had come to believe that one way to make men like them was to portray themselves as willing and eager sexual partners. Frequently, they did not perceive sexual acts as mutually satisfying but had seen them as gratifying to the man. This is not to say that these women did not enjoy sexual relations because frequently they reported that they did; however, the motivation was more toward satisfying the man's needs rather than their own.

Another pattern we have observed is sexual revictimization in-\
volving rape or rape attempts. Many of the women in our groups have experienced such attacks. Herman (1981) and Russell (1986) report similar findings. Russell's explanation of this fact is that it is often a product of dangers they encountered when running away from their abusive homes "and/or . . . low self-esteem and lack of assertiveness which render them vulnerable to sexual exploitation by predatory males" (p. 134). This is consistent with our experience. Whatever the reason for such revictimization, deep feelings of vulnerability and fear result.

SEXUAL ORIENTATION AND PREFERENCE

Although there is little objective evidence supporting abuse as a causative factor in the development of sexual orientation and preference, group leaders need to be sensitive to the fact that many survivors of sexual abuse struggle with the issue of sexual orientation and the relationship of their abuse to this issue. Some of them are concerned that there may be a causative relationship. Below are cited our clinical observations and some studies that have explored this relationship. Although in no way definitive, they are provided to assist leaders in thinking about this issue.

Maltz and Holman (1987) and Johnson and Shrier (1985) indicate that childhood sexual abuse may influence adult sexual preference and orientation in both women and men. Johnson and Shrier found that a high percentage of boys who were sexually abused by men do indicate a homosexual preference as adults. Maltz and Holman speculate that there are two groups of formerly abused women who exhibit a homosexual orientation: those who are lesbians who are also incest survivors, and those who may be heterosexual or bisexual but have chosen a lesbian lifestyle as part of their healing.

We have observed a number of women in our groups who seem to fit into this latter category relative to sexual preference. These women were withdrawn and anxious around men. They expressed varying degrees of fear related to developing relationships with men that might eventually result in sexual contact. What seems to have occurred is that the experience of precocious sexual contact or intercourse was so painful and frightening that, as adults, these women chose to avoid contact or close relationships with men.

Johnson and Shrier's (1985) study found that a high percentage of boys who were sexually abused by men exhibited homosexual orientation as adults. There are much less data on sexual abuse of males, and our groups represent a relatively small sample of males. Nevertheless, we have seen men confused about their sexual orientation, convinced that they *must* be gay because they were abused by males. We suspect that male survivors fall into groups similar to those Maltz and Holman identified above for women.

We have also seen confusion over sexual identity in men who have had violent, physically abusive fathers and passive, though warm and nurturing mothers. The male survivor may identify with his mother and become effeminate or even homosexual as a way of disowning any relationship with, or similarity to, the violent, aggressive father.

Another dynamic may occur when there is an aggressive mother and passive father. In one case in our experience, a male group member acted out the trauma of sexual (coupled with physical) abuse by his mother in the opposite manner. Rather than choose a female standard for behavior, he became sexually active at an early age and continued into mid-adulthood, seeking sexual encounters as conquests to reaffirm his manhood and sense of control and power over his sexual life. Most often, these sexual experiences were devoid of love and seemed related to power and control. They were more a confirmation of his sexual competence and male identity, and an acting out against a dominant, hostile mother rather than acts of intimacy for the purpose of gaining closeness to another person. Once this man recalled the sexual abuse and made the link to his previous experience, he was able to work toward freeing himself of the compulsion to seek out sexual conquests.

SEXUAL AROUSAL, RESPONSE, AND SATISFACTION

Maltz and Holman (1987) indicate that female incest survivors tend to experience more sexual problems than do women who are not abused, especially in the areas of sexual desire and sexual pleasure. Jehu (1988) identifies several categories of sexual dysfunction: phobia/aversion, dissatisfaction, impaired motivation, impaired arousal, impaired orgasm, dyspareunia, and vaginismus. These may be the result of various causes: organic factors, mood disturbances, and interpersonal problems. However, sexual stress resulting from early sexual abuse is a common component of sexual dysfunction. We have heard group members, both female and male, express great anxiety, aversion, and fear as well as dissatisfaction about what should have been fulfilling sexual experiences. A significant source of intimacy and pleasure has been distorted. Not as much data are available on the incidence of sexual abuse of males as there are for females, and we have not encountered a large sample of men in our groups. However, there is reason to believe that the frequency of this experience is greater than previously believed. Surveys of nonclinical populations find ranges of 3% to 10% of American men who were sexually victimized as children (Finkelhor, 1979; Fritz, Stoll, & Wagner, 1981; Gagnon, 1965; Kercher & McShane, 1984). Finkelhor, Hotaling, Lewis, and Smith (1990) found a prevalence rate of 16% for males. Furthermore, Nielsen (1983) reports that professionals involved in child abuse projects indicate that boys comprise 25% to 35% of their caseloads. A review of clinical studies (DeJong, Emmett, & Hervada, 1982) found male sex abuse rates between 11% and 17%. What is clear is that boys are unlikely to report these experiences because of the same fear of personal harm common to female victims, but they also are afraid that they will be held responsible because "real boys" should have been able to resist, or else they were supposed to "want it." Victimization "violates the male ethic of self-reliance, and also raises the stigma of homosexuality" (Bolton, Morris, & MacEachron, 1989, p. 39).

❏ Dissociation, Flashbacks, and Nightmares

Dissociation is a normal human response to a traumatic event. In the case of an emergency or life-threatening situation, use of dissociation may be imperative to effective action. For example, if your child is seriously injured, it may be critical to saving his or her life that you respond quickly, efficiently, and without emotion. In this case, you dissociate yourself from your feelings. It is only later, after the emergency is over, that you allow the feelings of fear, loss, or anger to surface and be experienced. Only then is it safe to feel your feelings and, it is hoped, receive comfort and support.

For many child victims of chronic, violent, physical or sexual abuse, dissociation becomes a primary coping defense. The abusive experience is so frightening, so painful, so utterly out of their control that they cannot possibly process it at the time. As Herman (1992) states,

> Traumatic reactions occur when action is of no avail. When neither resistance nor escape is possible, the human system of self-defense becomes overwhelmed and disorganized. . . . Traumatic events produce profound and lasting changes in physiological arousal, emotion, cognition, and memory. Moreover, traumatic events may sever these normally integrated functions from one another. (p. 34)

Thus, an individual may later either experience intense emotions but have no memory of the traumatic event, or have a clear memory but no emotional response. A third possibility is that the person is amnesic to the experience and only aware of it because of another person's report.

Unfortunately, in the case of intrafamilial abuse, when the traumatic event is over, the child does not have someone to talk to to make sense of the event and integrate it, nor does he or she have the luxury of experiencing the feelings and being comforted or reassured. In most cases, the abuse just keeps occurring and dissociation becomes the ongoing strategy for survival.

In practice, use of dissociation by many adult survivors of childhood abuse covers the full range of the continuum, including periodic daydreaming or "zoning out" of the present when anxiety levels start to rise, separating oneself from one's feelings (shutting down or numbing), blocking out information about one's experiences (amnesia), and creation of internal entities to hold certain memories or feelings (dissociative identity disorder). Group leaders can expect that dissociation may frequently occur during the group therapy process.

Flashbacks and nightmares also can be anticipated as part of the recovery process as dissociated material is triggered and the survivor struggles to bring this information to the surface for processing and resolution. Simply stated, a flashback is a reexperiencing of a traumatic event. Flashbacks may consist of momentary glimpses of the past, almost like snapshots that are passed quickly before one's eyes. Or they may entail a full-blown reexperiencing of a major trauma complete with visual, auditory, and tactile sensations. Sometimes, clients will report strong physiological or emotional reactions to seemingly harmless stimuli. These may be identified later as emotional flashbacks; that is, the memory of the event is not consciously present (i.e., it is dissociated), but the body, mind, or emotions remember at some level and react.

For example, one woman had an intense fear reaction whenever she was near an aquarium. Any time she was near an aquarium, she would begin to experience high anxiety and fear coupled with shortness of breath and rapid breathing—a reaction resembling a panic attack. She would become so uncomfortable that she would have to leave. During the course of her therapy, she was finally able to remember a time from childhood when her father sexually molested her on the couch in his den. Resting on the shelf behind the couch was a large aquarium filled with tropical fish, her focal point during the abuse. After she was able to make the connection, she was able to understand her apparently irrational fear response.

Survivors may also report somatic complaints. Many women describe sharp, physical pains around their genital area or in their vaginas, or intense pain in their legs or back that cannot be attributed to any medical problem or through any other logical explanation. Some survivors describe the sensation of being held down or of having insects crawling on them. These mysterious bodily responses (or "body memories") may come and go without an understanding as to what has triggered them. Often, they are followed by a memory from the past that clarifies what the body was trying to disclose.

One needs to be aware that anything (a place, object, time of day, season of the year, article of clothing, odor, word, voice tone, etc.)

can serve as a trigger for reexperiencing past experiences. At times, these full or partial flashbacks are so vivid and terrifying that the adult becomes disoriented and out of touch with the present. Further discussion of responding to flashbacks in the group setting is provided in Chapter 4.

Many survivors also experience intense, frightening nightmares and night terrors. If the adult has had no previous memory of sexual or physical abuse and begins to get in touch with these past experiences, flashbacks and nightmares may occur as part of the process of working through and attempting to resolve the experience. Blocked memories may be triggered during the group session as members disclose incidents from their pasts. Such selective amnesia of memories of traumatic incidents is a key symptom of posttraumatic stress disorder, sometimes called "delayed stress syndrome" because the reactions—and recollections of trauma—come many years after the actual event.

Previously, we (Leehan & Wilson, 1985) suggested that the symptoms displayed by adult survivors of abuse might be best understood in the context of posttraumatic stress disorder. We argued that this diagnosis was useful because it allowed the group leader to view the symptom patterns manifested by survivors as a whole system related to, and stemming from, each person's history of abuse.

Since that time, Finkelhor and Browne (1985) and Friedrich (1990) have developed comprehensive models that seek to describe the long-term effects of childhood sexual abuse and to explain the dynamics of how childhood sexual abuse creates disturbances in affective functioning and distortions in cognitive belief systems that lead to maladaptive behavioral coping strategies.

Additionally, Herman (1992) has called for a new diagnosis for the syndrome that plagues survivors of prolonged, repeated trauma. She calls it "complex posttraumatic stress disorder" and states that "responses to trauma are best understood as a spectrum of conditions rather than as a single disorder" (p. 119). She emphasizes the importance of considering the entire symptom pattern and points out the history of misdiagnosis and mistreatment that is prevalent for many survivors of childhood abuse because of the complexity and diversity of their symptoms. As she states, "Survivors of childhood abuse often accumulate many different diagnoses before the underlying problem of a complex posttraumatic syndrome is recognized" (p. 23).

❏ Taking a Multidimensional Approach

We recommend that as potential group leaders seek to provide diagnoses and treatment plans for survivors of child abuse and neglect, they should consider the cluster of presenting symptoms as a unified whole and employ a multidimensional intervention strategy that recognizes the cognitive, emotional, and behavioral effects of the abuse experience. In addition, these treatment plans need to be sensitive to and respectful of the coping strategies that adult survivors have learned to employ.

First, a multidimensional approach must include major challenges to the survivor's learned belief system about oneself and the world. The goal of this cognitive restructuring is to assist the survivor in developing a more accurate self-image and a more realistic, and hopefully optimistic, view of the relationship of others to oneself.

In addition to intervention at the cognitive level, reeducation in the handling of one's feelings and emotions must be provided. Often, this will require starting at square one by defining and identifying feelings and progressing to the stage of learning new ways to express feelings that are satisfying, provide relief, and are generally acceptable and appropriate.

Finally, there needs to be a therapeutic component that teaches the skills and behaviors needed for competent, effective day-to-day living. Dysfunctional behavioral strategies (that may well have been adaptive for survival in the abusive family of origin) need to be identified, understood, and replaced over time with behaviors that are applicable to the present life circumstances of the survivor.

Whereas the cognitive reframing, the emotional efficacy, and the new behavioral strategies can be achieved effectively through individual therapy, use of a group therapy approach often hastens the recovery process. It is more difficult to hold on to a negative self-image based on one's "badness" stemming from "things that happened to me in childhood" when one begins to care about and respect others who have experienced similar abuse. The belief that "I am unlovable or worthless" becomes less believable when one is confronted week after week by caring, supportive people who know "the awful truth about me" and love one in spite of it.

Struggling to identify and discuss what "I am feeling" becomes more bearable when there are others available to listen who "know where I'm coming from" because they have been there themselves. Practicing new behaviors, especially in the area of interpersonal relationships, becomes less painful and embarrassing when there are others who are "just as awkward and clumsy" with whom one can practice and with whom one can laugh (or cry) at mistakes and failings.

Thus, it becomes possible for survivors to believe that it is safe to trust others, their self-esteem tends to increase and is constantly reinforced, and the feelings of stigmatization created by the traumatic events are diminished. Lives become more controllable, and feelings of power start to replace the helplessness and vulnerability of the past.

❏ Summary

In this chapter, we have offered definitions of child abuse and neglect and have discussed the long-term effects of such treatment. We have emphasized that these long-term effects constitute an interrelated system of symptoms requiring a multidimensional treatment plan. In the next chapter, we will discuss the goals of group therapy for adult survivors of childhood abuse and illustrate through case studies how group intervention can provide the treatment needed. Later chapters will examine the advantages and cautions to be observed in conducting such groups as well as the strategies to be employed.

2

Goals for Therapy Groups

"I feel almost guilty to say this, but it is so good to hear what has happened to all of you. For the first time I don't feel so alone."
—Ned, 34-year-old businessman

"For the first time I don't have to worry about shocking people. You all have had equally horrible experiences."
—Mary, 25-year-old legal secretary

The goals of groups for adult survivors are directly related to the individual and interpersonal problems discussed in the previous chapter. It is important that the group process intentionally address the needs of survivors and develop a milieu that both challenges the participants to deal with the long-range effects of their abuse and supports them in the process. In this chapter, we will discuss the general goals and orientation for such groups. Later, we will consider specific strategies and the roles the leaders must take to facilitate the attainment of these goals.

❏ **The Process of Healing**

We (Leehan & Wilson, 1985) formerly identified a common process through which adult survivors need to go in order to heal the
effects of their abusive childhoods. This process includes acknowledging the abusive experience, processing the emotional response,
identifying the effects of the abuse, and learning strategies to deal
with these effects. Although this process is fairly consistent, it does
not flow smoothly in one direction. There are frequent new begin-
nings as different aspects of the abuse experience are identified and
confronted.

ACCEPTING THE ABUSE

The first step is that survivors *actually acknowledge the fact of their
abuse.* This is not as simple as it may seem. As stated previously,
sometimes victims do not remember any of their abuse, or remember only certain aspects of it (e.g., they remember physical beatings,
but not sexual assaults). Even when they do remember the violence,
they also must be able to label it as abuse. They must acknowledge
that the beatings they received were not typical and acceptable
methods of parental discipline. What happened to them was excessive and inappropriate, but it was something for which they were
not to blame. They must be able to distinguish their responsibility
from that of their parents.

Naturally, this step must have begun before people even enter a
group. At least, they must have identified themselves as having been
victims of child abuse, even if they are not conscious of all the facets
of their experience. The former victims also must have determined
who was responsible for the abuse before they enter a group. They
must have moved beyond the need to attribute blame for what
happened to the stage of learning to cope with the effects of their
experience.

PROCESSING THE EMOTIONAL RESPONSE TO ABUSE

Once that principally intellectual process of recognizing and acknowledging the nature of their abuse has been accomplished, survivors must move to the next step in the process: *identifying and resolving their emotional response to those experiences.* This, too, is not as simple as it may seem. It raises many conflicting emotions.

In most cases, the people responsible for the abuse were parents or people close to the survivors, the very people society has told them they are to love and respect. The former victims often want desperately to feel genuine affection for those people who abused them or failed to protect them. Their hope of someday achieving a loving, intimate relationship with their parents often has been their only source of consolation. They fear that if they fully acknowledge their anger and disappointment, their last vestige of hope for a "real" family relationship will be destroyed. It will be the end of their chances for a normal family experience. Therefore, survivors frequently provide numerous rationalizations for their parents' behavior, and they block, minimize, and deny their own emotional reactions to what happened to them.

Besides this continuing hope for a normal family life, abuse survivors also find this step in the process difficult because it involves acknowledging and expressing intense feelings of anger and resentment. In other parts of this book, we will discuss at great length the problems and fears related to this as well as methods for achieving resolution.

RECOGNIZING THE EFFECTS OF THE ABUSE

The next step in the process, and again a more intellectual one, is that the former victims must *recognize the continuing impact their abusive pasts have on their present behavior.* This means that they must realize how that past experience colors their perceptions of and responses to people and situations in their present. They need to learn to recognize when their present responses are inappropriate. Their inappropriate responses may range from inordinate fear of anyone in authority to mistrust of everyone they meet, from fear of success to excessive striving for perfection, from insecurity in social situations to problems with sexuality. The possible reactions are numerous and varied.

As part of this step, adult survivors need to learn to distinguish between situations in their past and similar experiences in the present. They must learn to differentiate people who have authority over them in the present from abusive people in their past. They must begin to recognize and control the transference that may be occurring between their past and their present.

LEARNING NEW STRATEGIES

The final step in the process is for abuse survivors to *learn and apply alternate methods of performing tasks, relating to people, and responding to situations.* This step grows naturally but slowly out of the previous steps. Once the inappropriateness of previous methods is acknowledged, the former victims can explore new options, choose new behaviors, and practice applying them in various situations. However, they are only free to do this after they have recognized and resolved some of the previously discussed influences of their abusive experience. Only by confronting the various intellectual and emotional components of their abusive past are these adults able to achieve control over their emotional and behavioral responses to the present.

As we said at the beginning of this section, these steps are consistent but do not always flow continually in one direction. As new issues arise and as these adults confront different aspects of their experiences, the process must be started again and the sources of present problems traced to the previous experiences that are influencing the present feelings and behaviors. The important thing is that the leaders know where the group members are in the process so that they can provide the most helpful guidance and keep the group's process on track.

To facilitate this healing process, there are six basic goals for groups.

Goals for Groups

1. To break down the sense of isolation that former abuse victims experience
2. To provide a safe, supportive, and understanding environment in which members can share past and present experiences, express feelings, experiment with new behavior(s), and develop close personal relationships
3. To provide a consistent, predictable environment in which members can learn that they can trust others and that they themselves are trustworthy and entitled to self-esteem
4. To provide opportunities for group problem solving to help members learn to make decisions and take greater control of their lives
5. To enable and encourage members to express long-repressed emotions so they can overcome the fears they have associated with the experiencing of emotions, and learn appropriate ways of expressing feelings
6. To provide a setting in which members can learn and practice interpersonal communication skills that enable them to meet their personal needs

---

These group goals relate to creating a group environment and process that enable individual members to enter into their own healing process. The attainment of these goals provides a context within which members can examine their abuse experience and its impact on their lives and develop new methods of resolving and managing those effects. Each goal will be discussed individually, although they are not totally discrete. There is overlap, and achievement of one goal often is prerequisite to identification of and action toward achieving another.

❏ Goal 1: Breaking the Sense of Isolation

To break down the sense of isolation that former abuse victims experience.

As we have stated, adult survivors rarely have shared or discussed their experience of abuse with other people. This is partly because of the general lack of communication in their homes. Furthermore, as children or adolescents, when the abuse was most severe, they were repeatedly threatened to be silent about the abusive behavior of their parents. Many were led to believe that the abuse was punishment that they deserved and received because they were "bad."

Those who finally could no longer endure the abuse, or who became aware that it was not a normal family interaction and did attempt to discuss their situation with others, often were not believed. Frequently, they were revictimized by the person they had chosen to trust as confidante. They were chastised for telling "lies" about their "lovely parents." Most of the adults in our groups thus far grew up in the 1950s and 1960s when society did not permit discussion of child abuse or recognize it as a problem of "nice" people.

We know today that child abuse is a crime that cuts across all socioeconomic classes and racial and ethnic backgrounds (Gelles & Cornell, 1985; Straus, Gelles, & Steinmetz, 1980). But very few people, even mental health professionals, knew this 20, 30, or 40 years ago when today's adults were young. Outsiders to whom abused children tried to confide their experiences generally tried to deny what they were hearing and refused, or were reluctant, to become involved in other people's family lives. In the rare case that someone was willing to listen and wanted to provide assistance, there were few, if any, resources available to aid the abuse victim. Often, the only help he or she received was the relief felt at finally telling someone and being believed. Thus, for the most part, the silence and sense of isolation were reinforced by others outside the family unit.

Thus, a major focus of this goal is to get the group members to feel that it is all right to finally disclose those experiences they have carefully hidden from others all their lives. Some people find it difficult to share their stories, even in a group established for that purpose. However, we have seen repeatedly that as soon as one person breaks the barrier of silence and begins to share his or her past experience, the others quickly follow, expressing relief at finally being able to "tell their stories." The extent of detail varies from person to person. Some seem to need to "play out" specific past events or memories; others speak only in the most general terms.

Of course, some find the experience of sharing frightening or shameful. The "rule of silence" was so well learned in their families that they need to be continually reassured.

The actual telling of these abusive experiences to a sensitive, nonjudgmental, supportive group functions as a catharsis and begins the process of breaking down the defenses that have kept these individuals insulated, as well as isolated, for most of their lives. It is a painful, difficult sharing, not a swapping of horror stories. As such, it is one of the greatest risks the group members have taken in their lives. After members begin to share and the episodes of abuse have been acknowledged by others, the former abuse victims can begin to move toward a sense of closeness to and trust of others and a greater understanding of themselves.

❏ Goal 2: Providing a Supportive Environment

To provide a safe, supportive and understanding environment in which members can share past and present experiences, express feelings, experiment with new behavior(s), and develop close personal relationships.

This goal is closely related to the first because the only way to make it really possible for these adults to share the experiences of the past and break through the shells that keep them isolated from others is to provide a safe place and the opportunity and impetus to talk about painful and difficult issues. One way in which the group leaders set the stage and attempt to build the basis for trust is to begin the first group meeting with a discussion of the ground rules or guidelines that are critical to the group's process.

Ground Rules

Rules of Participation

1. Members will actively participate to the best of their ability, sharing their history and present struggles as well as listening and responding to others.
2. Although all are encouraged to share, all also have the right to refuse to talk at certain times.
3. Regular and prompt attendance is necessary for continuity and trust within the group.

Rules of Safety

The expression of strong emotions (anger, sadness, anxiety, etc.) is expected and encouraged, but no physical or verbal violence directed at people is allowed.

Rules of Confidentiality

1. All matters discussed in the group are confidential.
2. Contact among group members between sessions is acceptable but discussion of matters related to the group should not occur.

RULES OF PARTICIPATION

The first requirement is that group members agree to be active participants within the group process. Although this may seem so obvious as to not need mentioning, we have found that many abuse victims find it incredibly difficult to talk about themselves in a serious, honest manner. Most of them would like very much to be open with their feelings and free to discuss their problems, but years of experience have taught them that it is not safe to talk about those things because they become vulnerable. Thus, one of the responsibilities each group member assumes is to make his or her own effort to share and to provide encouragement and support to others' efforts.

The group leaders must remind the members frequently that they will be encouraged, and even pushed, to disclose and explore issues and problems. One of the ground rules with respect to this "pushing" is that if a person is truly unable to talk about an issue, or if the discussion becomes too frightening or painful, the rest of the group will back off until a later time. As one group member stated very aptly, "I know I need to be on the hot seat sometimes, and I know I'll learn and grow from it, but sometimes it gets too hot and I'm afraid I'll get burned. Then I need to stop for a while." This stance seems fair to group members because they know well that unresolved issues will continue to clamor for understanding and resolution.

RULES OF SAFETY

The second ground rule affirms the appropriateness of exploring and expressing strong emotions within the group as part of the therapeutic process but guarantees the safety of all members. Survivors have all too often experienced that the expression of strong emotion, especially anger, means violence. Therefore, they avoid all such emotion. It is important to assure them that exploring emotions is an acceptable task, but that they and others will be kept safe. It is possible to be emotional without being abusive.

RULES OF CONFIDENTIALITY

The third set of requirements relates to the need for confidentiality. Given the problems with trust that survivors experience, confidentiality is a key issue requiring discussion, and it has two aspects. First, group leaders must emphasize that, as in all therapeutic settings, the issues, problems, and feelings expressed and discussed in the group are not to be discussed with nongroup members. Second, matters discussed in the group may not be discussed privately by members outside the group sessions.

CONTACT OUTSIDE THE GROUP—PROS AND CONS

To ensure this latter form of confidentiality, some group leaders rule out all contact among group members between sessions (Vannicelli, 1989). In accordance with others (Yalom, 1985), we have chosen not to do so. In fact, we encourage members to contact one another for friendship and support. For some group members, these out-of-group contacts provide opportunities for much-needed practice in friendship and social skills. They also serve to counteract the loneliness and isolation felt by many survivors. Sometimes, these contacts even function as confidence-building experiences when two or three group members decide to try something new or go somewhere together, taking risks that none of them would try on his or her own. With participants' permission, we even provide a list of group members and their phone numbers.

In addition, one of the things that survivors need to learn is how to establish caring relationships and how to ask for and give support. To declare group members "off limits" for that process eliminates a potentially significant group of people with whom they can learn to interact and from whom they can gain support. As individual members struggle with the anxieties and frustrations of resolving the impact of their abuse, who can be a better source of encouragement than one who has gone through the same trial? What can be a better boost for a struggling survivor's self-esteem than to have another group member say, "What you said on the phone last night really helped me"?

This is not to say that such interactions are without potential problems. Not all advice from other survivors constitutes pearls of wisdom. Not all relationships are guaranteed to be healthy. Group leaders will need to monitor these contacts to ensure that they are helpful and supportive to the individual members and the comaraderie and functioning of the group. Education about proper relationship boundaries may be necessary. Helping group members learn how to set clear limits with one another about what they are willing and able to offer in a relationship, such as when they will be available or what kind of support or assistance they can provide, is good practice for relationships outside the group.

In some instances, group leaders may need to set the boundaries. For example, dating and sexual relationships between group members are not acceptable.

Problems for the group as a whole that may arise from such contacts may take several forms. If members discuss group issues in private meetings outside the group, there is the potential for such discussion to interfere with group cohesiveness and the work that needs to be done together. For example, in all groups, there are occasions when time runs out and issues or problems are left unresolved. This can result in a great deal of anxiety for group members, who all tend to experience intense guilt feelings if the group does not "go well." This guilt and anxiety may cause one member to call or meet with another member in an attempt to gain understanding or at least diminish the anxiety.

This discussion can be very useful if it results in the resolution of a problem that has arisen in the group between these same two members. When this occurs, we require that at the next meeting, these members share with the others some information about the resolution so that it is clear that the problem has been dealt with and no longer needs attention. Such sharing also helps the other members learn how such resolutions can be attained.

Outside discussion also can become harmful when one member has a problem with another member and, instead of dealing with that member, calls on a third member for support. The danger in this process becomes apparent at the next group meeting when the two people align themselves against the third member. Such alliances are destructive both to the individual's growth and to the group's life. They should be confronted and discouraged. It is important to remember that such alliances occur because of the fear and incompetence a group member may feel at having to stand up to (and usually this means disagree with) another person.

Although there may be problems with such outside contacts between group members, and leaders do need to be alert to them, the discussion of a resolution of such issues can be an important part of the therapeutic process for survivors. Critical issues in their healing involve learning to define personal boundaries and learning to establish relationships with others that are different from the triangulated and scapegoating experiences of their families.

After establishing the basic ground rules, we ask that group members suggest any guidelines that they would like the group to follow. This provides impetus for a discussion of members' fears, concerns, and reservations about being part of the group. Talking about these fears and concerns tends to provide a natural lead-in to the discussion of the previous abuse experiences of group members. By this time, they have had a chance to relax somewhat and to get used to the leaders and other group members, and many are finally ready to disclose their past history.

TALKING ABOUT THE ABUSE EXPERIENCE

Group members talk about their abuse experiences in many ways. As we have said, some simply say that they were physically abused by their father or mother; others go into more detail about specific past events. The degree of detail does not seem so important initially as the actual "public" statement of having been a victim of abuse. The nonverbal expressions of relief after the disclosure seem to shout. Body postures become more relaxed. Tension fades from faces. Often, group members will laugh and joke about how afraid they were to tell of their past and will express their surprise at how easy it was once they got started. Occasionally, someone will cry with relief and joy.

Although this display of emotion is not surprising, what seems unusual is the immediate natural empathy that seems to flow between group members. The expression of this painful common bond seems to draw the group together and begin the process of creating a safe, supportive, and understanding environment. Although each person's abuse experience is unique, the feelings of being alone in the world and being the only one with this terrible stigma seem to fade as members realize that there are others who have been victimized and have endured the shame and pain of abuse. This insight helps group members learn the process of caring and providing support over time as they get to know one another better.

Consistency becomes a key component in the successful achievement of the second goal and is the focus of the third goal. Because of the ever-present chaos in the abusive home, establishing a consistent base in the lives of these adult survivors is a critical goal that warrants individual attention.

❏ Goal 3: Providing Consistency to Promote Trust

To provide a consistent, predictable environment in which members can learn that they can trust others and that they themselves are trustworthy and entitled to self-esteem.

One characteristic of the abusive family is the inconsistency of parental behavior (Gelles, 1987; Justice & Duncan, 1976; Justice & Justice, 1976). As we have said, this inconsistency and the resulting inability of abused children to predict the consequences of their own behavior are primary reasons that abuse victims have great difficulty in learning to trust themselves and others. Therefore, we have found that it is important to stress consistency and order in the group setting.

CONSISTENCY OF GROUP LEADER RESPONSE

Consistency of response, especially from group leaders, is critical. Group leaders need to be constant in their openness to and empathy for members of the group. They must be willing to listen to members' accounts of their abuse experiences, sensitive to and understanding of the many intense emotions that may pour forth with this recounting, and supportive of members as they move toward healing from the past experiences.

As the group progresses and members become more open to expressing fears, needs, problems, and weaknesses, there is a constant need for reassurance and support. Inattention or unresponsiveness will be interpreted quickly as lack of caring and rejection. Group leaders will be tested repeatedly to see if they deviate from a consistent, supportive response. Often, this "testing" takes the form of baiting in which group members intentionally engage in regressive or other inappropriate attention-getting behavior just to see how the other members and the leaders will react.

Because this behavior tends to be self-defeating, it is important to confront the person directly while at the same time providing reassurance that he or she is still likable and worthwhile. We emphasize the inappropriateness of the *behavior*, not the *person*. The following example will illustrate how one such instance of self-defeating behavior was handled effectively:

Mark had been a member of two successive groups over a period of about 1½ years. During most of this time, he had rarely spoken, although he had been encouraged often to participate. Finally, during the second year, another group member expressed her frustration and annoyance at his reluctance to share his thoughts and feelings with the group. Something finally clicked for Mark, and, although hesitant, he began to offer more and more comments at each group meeting.

At one meeting, nearly the entire time was devoted to helping Mark with a problem he was facing. He was tense and nervous, but he seemed to enjoy being the center of attention and was open to comments and suggestions. Toward the end of the meeting, he expressed his appreciation to the members and told them how helpful the session had been for him.

During the next two group meetings, the focus was primarily on other group members, and Mark reverted to his more typical behavior of limited verbal participation, although he remained attentive and interested in the group activity. By the third week, his verbal participation was limited to one- or two-word responses, and his nonverbal behavior included very little or no eye contact and a lack of attention to what others said. When asked to participate, he simply replied, "Pass." It became clear that he was using this regressive behavior to manipulate the other group members into paying attention to him. Several members became angry and started confronting him with his "childish" behavior.

At this point, the group leader intervened and pointed out how the behavior was self-defeating and was not helping Mark get the positive response and attention he really wanted and needed. The leader emphasized that she understood that it was difficult for Mark to ask directly for what he wanted, but that one purpose of the group was to help members learn more effective behaviors for getting what they want or need.

She also stressed that everyone liked and cared about Mark, but that his regressive behavior was not acceptable. She encouraged

Mark to take a risk, be more assertive, and ask for support instead of attempting to manipulate the other members. The other members' anger was defused, and they were able to be supportive and to make sincere efforts to draw him out. Mark gradually became more assertive.

As illustrated in the above scenario, a key issue in consistency is walking the fine line of providing reassurance and support while not allowing ineffective or self-defeating behaviors.

Providing structure and order is another important way to promote consistency in the group. It also serves to ease tension and raise the comfort level of group members. As previously indicated, by spelling out group guidelines, outlining the content and structure of the groups, and clarifying group goals, a sound foundation for consistency in group functioning is laid.

CONSISTENT ATTENDANCE

Consistency in attendance is also required. Initially, we ask group members to make a commitment to attend four consecutive meetings. This commitment is extremely important. All groups take some time to form and develop cohesion so that members feel comfortable. We have found that members need a minimum of four meetings to attain the comfort level necessary to give the group a "fair trial." After the four meetings have passed, we discuss with group members how they feel the group is going. We examine factors about which members have concerns (e.g., topics that have not been examined, the amount of time given to people or issues). Modifications are made as needed, and a longer commitment of 2 to 3 months is determined. Another reassessment of group progress is made at the end of that time.

Group leaders need to be aware of one important fact related to this commitment to attend meetings. For an adult survivor, the hardest part of being a group member may be coming to the meeting. For many, this is the first attempt to act counter to their past behavior of refusing to acknowledge their abuse experience. One woman, for example, came to the third meeting of a group and admitted that she had come to the first two meetings at the appointed time, but had stayed in her car the entire two hours. After each meeting, one of the group leaders had called to ask if she was still interested in participating, told her the next week's meeting time, and encouraged her to come. She never admitted she had been sitting outside in the parking lot. Only at the third attempt could she overcome her fear and anxiety and leave her car to join the group.

Leaders must repeatedly stress that each member is important to the group process and should encourage members to contact one another the day before a meeting to ensure full attendance. This procedure also helps to hasten and strengthen the development of group cohesion.

Another way to ensure consistency is to insist that if at any time a member wishes to leave the group, he or she must attend at least one more meeting to discuss the reasons for terminating. This ensures that the remaining members do not feel personally rejected. It often happens that the departing member's reasons for wishing to terminate can be resolved and continued participation can be ensured. Further discussion of termination issues will be considered in Chapter 4.

CONSISTENT STRUCTURE

Consistency in the structure of each session is also helpful. We begin each meeting with a brief opportunity for each person to summarize positive and negative events from the previous week as a way to "touch base." Leaders ask members whether there are issues or concerns that they want the group to deal with that day. This helps the leaders to determine how much time may be allotted to each person and whose concerns are the most pressing and require immediate attention.

Although this technique is generally very useful for providing consistency and structure to the group meeting and for having concerns expressed at the start, problems do occasionally arise. It is often very difficult for abuse victims to talk about problem areas or negative events in their lives, and once they do manage to bring up these concerns, it is also difficult to "turn them off" or "put them on hold" until later in the session.

For example, one group member who had extremely hostile feelings toward her mother finally started to talk about her anger and hostility at the beginning of one session. She began to express these feelings in relation to a recent incident that had brought them to the surface. After several minutes of discussion, we felt it was necessary to go on and "touch base" with the other group members. Thus, we asked if this was something she wanted to come back to later in the meeting. She gave a begrudging "yes" and we continued around the circle.

Later, when we tried to get her to talk about her mother again, she refused. This resulted in frustration for us as well as for the other group members. When confronted with her unwillingness to share, the woman finally burst forth with anger at us and the group for not letting her finish once she had started. For her, it was too painful to "put her feelings on hold" and raise the issue twice in one meeting.

Obviously, in instances like this, it may be necessary to forego the usual group technique of "touching base." But if the structure is given up completely and the group becomes more loose in this way, group leaders may find that the more loquacious members monopolize the meetings and the reticent members do not get the regular opportunities they need to speak.

The first three goals we have discussed relate to establishing conditions within the group setting that enable the group to function in a way that fosters cognitive changes in the members' belief systems and attitudes. More specifically, the premise is that once a safe, supportive, consistent environment has been established, the members will be able to explore their irrational and negative beliefs about themselves. From this will come insights that lead to greater self-acceptance and a changed attitude toward themselves and other people.

The next three goals are designed to help members use these new insights and changed attitudes to make specific changes in their behavior. These goals promote skill development in three areas: problem solving and decision making, appropriate expression of emotion, and effective communication with others.

❏ Goal 4: Providing Opportunities for Problem Solving

To provide opportunities for group problem solving to help members learn to make decisions and take greater control of their lives.

This goal relates specifically to two of the recurring problems of survivors that we discussed in the preceding chapters: the inability to generate and consider various alternative responses to problems, and feelings of helplessness and lack of control. Although the goal sounds very simple and straightforward, it is not so easy to achieve because it involves the use of several strategies.

First, a problem area must be chosen and clearly focused for discussion. Group members are then asked to discuss the ways in which they have tried—with varying degrees of success—to solve similar problems. As members suggest various techniques or behaviors, the leaders point out similarities in reacting to similar situations and ask which options may succeed, which may not, and why.

As the discussion progresses, the need for structure in the group again becomes evident because, as may be expected, members will frequently digress from the main issue. The main reason that these adults cannot solve problems or make decisions is that they cannot remain focused on a particular issue long enough to generate an effective solution or mode of behavior. Never having had an opportunity to generate, discuss, and implement effective responses to problems, they frequently settle on the first response that comes to mind—not always the best response—rather than considering and weighing the options.

Group discussion of alternative approaches to problem situations serves several purposes. First, it illustrates clearly that there are many ways to approach a problem or reach a decision. Second, members have an opportunity to debate and discuss the various alternatives, and, most important, they are able to project the consequences of various actions. This second step is essential for gaining control over one's life. As group members begin to imagine the probable success or failure of a given approach, they come to see that they do, in fact, have control over many of the events of their lives. They learn that certain behaviors will elicit fairly predictable responses from others—not everyone is like their inconsistent, unpredictable parents.

This knowledge or insight into one's own behavior and that of others leads to a new feeling of power and control over one's own destiny. Group members no longer perceive themselves as vulnerable, waiting victims ready to be pushed around by the actions and whims of others.

Furthermore, as the feelings of control become stronger, the need to make choices and consider alternatives becomes more important. The thought seems to be, "Now that I believe I have some control over my life, I had better make sure I learn which decisions and actions will best help me achieve what I want and need." Thus, the group helps each individual generate alternative approaches, discuss the probable effects of those alternatives, and provide support and reinforcement for the selection of the approach that is most likely to be effective. Members can then act on a decision by developing and implementing a plan.

If the approach chosen does not succeed, the group can help by providing reassurance and by considering what went wrong and why. Learning to engage in this kind of logical thought pattern and to translate it into specific action is a major accomplishment for former abuse victims.

Group leaders can have an important part to play in this process as role models. Members often find it helpful for leaders to describe their own decision-making patterns and discuss both successful and unsuccessful decisions. Members are able to see that they are not the only ones who make "wrong" or ineffective decisions: People who were not abused are also vulnerable and can make mistakes.

The process of decision making we have just described is very rational and linear. As anyone who has struggled with difficult and frightening decisions knows, decision making generally is not so clear-cut. Although it is possible to delineate a clear and rational step-by-step approach to making a decision or solving a problem, many emotions also are evoked that can confuse the process. This is the subject matter of the next goal.

❏ Goal 5: Learning to Express and Deal With Feelings

To enable and encourage members to express long-repressed emotions so that they can overcome the fears associated with the experiencing of emotions and learn appropriate ways of expressing feelings.

As we have stated, at the first meeting of a group we discuss the goals for groups. Although we explain all the goals, we especially emphasize this goal of enabling and encouraging members to express their emotions. We do this in part as a way to help members talk about their past experiences of abuse. Because these experiences are filled with great emotion, members need to know that it is all right if their feelings show as they speak of these past events.

We also emphasize this goal so that members know that they have the freedom to express any emotion and to say whatever they feel, even if their statements are filled with anger, hatred, or hostility. We continue to encourage this identification, acknowledgment, expression, and discussion of feelings at each meeting.

DISSOCIATED FEELINGS

Often when members finally do describe an incident from the past or present that would normally be accompanied by feelings of anger, pain, or guilt, there is a complete lack of affect in the voice and nonverbal expression of the speaker. Even when describing instances of brutal mistreatment or gross injustice, the person will be matter-of-fact and exhibit no affect, as if commenting on the weather. Generally, the account is restricted to a simple narration. Rarely does this person express or even allude to a feeling state associated with the experience.

Frequently, other members of the group are deeply affected by the description they have heard. They become angry or are moved to tears on behalf of the speaker. This "projective identification" serves three purposes. First, it models for the speaker the emotions he or she may not be able to express, showing him or her that such expression is safe and acceptable. In time, he or she may be able to imitate this modeling and express the feelings without prompting. Second, the compassionate response of others in the group offers the speaker the experience of others being concerned about and moved by his or her pain—something that generally did not occur in the home. Finally, the group members who have allowed themselves to respond so spontaneously to another's pain may begin to relate these feelings to their own pain about similar events that they have experienced and feel some compassion for themselves. Thus, it becomes an extremely powerful experience for all concerned.

To facilitate this process, opportunities must be provided for members to get in touch with the feelings bottled up inside them, and we must assure them that these feelings are natural, normal, and healthy responses to various experiences; that it is safe and acceptable to have and acknowledge feelings; and, most important, that there are ways to express feelings, even anger, that are not violent or destructive.

LEGITIMIZING FEELINGS

Legitimization of feelings begins by stating frequently within a group that all human beings have feelings in response to events in their lives, that these are normal and healthy responses to the environment, and that they are acceptable and allowable. Leaders must emphasize that there are no "bad" or "good" feelings; feelings simply exist. Certainly, some feeling states may be more pleasant than others, but this is a personal assessment or valuation.

What might be labeled "good" or "bad" and might result in reprisals by others is the *mode* of expressing one's feelings. The goal, in part, is to learn effective, satisfying, and appropriate means of expressing one's feelings. In the case of anger, nonviolent and constructive behaviors are suggested and practiced.

The legitimizing of feelings occurs as group members affirm the person's right to feel whatever feelings are experienced, no matter how intense or "unacceptable" they may seem. Furthermore, the group encourages and reinforces the labeling and "owning," or acknowledging, of the feelings as healthy.

It is helpful to trace a natural progression of feeling reactions to hypothetical events. This provides distancing, which allows the person to agree with the logic of this progression and even acknowledge that the feelings are legitimate and all right. For example, one might say, "If *(event or situation)* happened to me, I would feel *(insert feeling word)*, don't you agree?" The next step for the individual is to personalize and transfer this rational viewpoint and the legitimization of feelings to an actual experience in his or her own life.

"IT'S OKAY FOR THEM, BUT NOT FOR ME"

Sometimes, a form of denial can provide a major stumbling block to this process. Members end by saying, "It's all right for others to react that way, but it's not all right for me." Such statements must be challenged immediately by both leaders and members.

Group members must take part in this effort because in later sessions, virtually all of them eventually will try to deny that certain feelings are all right for them personally. If they have helped others to claim these same feelings, they will find it easier to identify their own incongruity and accept their feelings. The irrationality of saying "It's all right for everyone but me" eventually will make it easier for all members to allow themselves to acknowledge and express their feelings.

EXPRESSION OF FEELINGS

Once group members begin to acknowledge the feelings they have suppressed, or at least kept under tight rein, for years, the leaders need to move quickly to help them find effective ways to express these feelings. Leaders will notice that even in the case of pleasant affective states such as joy, satisfaction, or pride of accomplishment, acknowledgment and expression are tentative and guarded. One must understand that for these adults, it may be hard to believe that they can laugh or express joy and not have someone ridicule or disparage them or their accomplishment. They will learn that their expressions of joy may just as readily meet with positive reinforcement, support, and acclaim only after they have had many such favorable experiences. Strategies for effective expression of various emotions will be discussed in Chapter 4.

It took one group member 3 years to finally believe that he could count on the group to be accepting and supportive of him. He tested the group many times by acting in ways that he believed would arouse anger and draw negative reactions from members. As the group continued to accept him and respond in ways that were not hurtful to him or his self-esteem, he finally acknowledged that he trusted the members and felt safe coming to the group. He then admitted that he needed the group's support and felt comfortable with and accepted by the members. His relief at finally acknowledging and expressing his feelings toward the group was evident in both his more relaxed body posture and his increased verbal participation.

No matter how long it takes members to feel comfortable expressing their feelings, the support, assurance, and reinforcement given by other members and group leaders are instrumental in helping the person to internalize and believe in the importance of expressing emotions and continuing to strive for effective ways of dealing with them. This is an ongoing issue in any group.

❏ Goal 6: Learning Interpersonal Skills

To provide a setting in which members can learn and practice interpersonal communication skills that enable them to meet their personal needs.

Probably the most frequent complaint from group members is that they do not know how to make friends or talk to people. They say that they feel uncomfortable and anxious in social situations. They stumble over their words and say things they do not really mean. At worst, they become so immobilized that they cannot speak at all and eventually flee from the situation.

One quiet, soft-spoken young man comes to mind. At one of the initial group meetings where members were stating their individual goals, he finally spoke up and indicated his strong desire to learn good, effective communication skills. He recalled a home life with a strict, authoritarian father who knew little English and spoke to the children only when he was angry or was disciplining them. The young man's mother had died when he was young, and the other children were equally nonverbal.

Although the specifics of his family background are different from those of other abuse survivors, this home situation in which regular conversation or communication patterns are not learned or practiced is fairly typical. This deficiency in the home life makes it difficult for children to communicate with their peers and teachers at school, and they often become quiet and extremely introverted. This behavior persists in adulthood.

PROJECTION OF NEGATIVE SELF-BELIEFS ONTO OTHERS

Besides not having positive models or experiences of communication in their families, many abuse survivors have problems because they have strong feelings of inadequacy and low self-esteem, and they often believe that others share their negative perceptions. Only if they are made to talk about these perceptions and the opinions they attribute to others can they question the validity of their own assumptions and see themselves more realistically.

The following case study illustrates this point.

One male group member had decided to apply for a grant to cover the cost of some special training he needed. David had an initial interview with his company's aid officer and completed all the necessary paperwork. The official told him that the decision would take approximately 2 weeks. He enlisted the support of the two group leaders as references. They wrote and sent their letters, and the whole group waited eagerly for the response.

When no notification was forthcoming after 2 weeks, David called to inquire about the grant. He was told that the company was behind schedule in the processing of applications and that a decision had not been made. This continued for 2 weeks.

At this point, David scheduled another meeting with the aid officer. Prior to going to this meeting, one of the group leaders had an opportunity to talk with him. He was already feeling disappointed and certain that his application would be rejected. When the leader asked him why he was so sure of this, he said, "The woman doesn't like me." He had no documentation or rational reason for this belief.

The leader and David spent a great deal of time going over his previous contacts with this person, analyzing both the interview and the subsequent telephone contact. Nothing in her demeanor or her verbal responses suggested that she did not like him.

The leader offered several possible explanations for the woman's behavior, trying to show him that he had not necessarily been the cause of any negative affect she might have exhibited. David would say, for example, "She doesn't return my calls right away" or "She seemed like she wanted the interview to be over" as evidence that she did not like him. At this point, the leader asked David to suggest some reasons why the woman hadn't called back. He was able to admit begrudgingly that maybe she was very busy, especially if they were behind in their work, and that she had, in fact, called back.

Furthermore, the leader agreed that it was possible that the woman had wanted to close the interview but again asked David to consider other explanations. He was able to see that the reason could as easily have been that she had a lot of work to do or may have felt tired or harassed that day or was in trouble with her boss. The point was to help David understand that because he had done nothing to make the officer dislike him and because his behavior had been completely appropriate, there was no reason to assume that she had negative feelings toward him. This did, in fact, appear to have been the case because David did eventually receive his grant.

This example clearly illustrates several misbeliefs that survivors hold about themselves. Quite often, the reason that these people experience such great anxiety in social or other interpersonal situations is that they falsely attribute to other people the negative views of themselves that they learned in their families. Discussion of these misperceptions is generally useful in allaying some of the anxiety. If the members can come to believe to some degree that not everyone thinks they are stupid and that people do not make immediate judgments about their character on the basis of a first meeting, they can enter into such situations with greater self-confidence.

COUNTERACTING NEGATIVE SELF-BELIEFS

Within the group, we ask the members to share their impressions of one another. When they hear repeatedly that other people are "just like me" and feel the same incompetence and anxiety, they finally begin to believe that they are not hopelessly retarded socially. This is especially true when they hear others whom they like and respect, and perceive as being relaxed and comfortable, admit that they feel nervous and inadequate in interpersonal situations.

As members gain insight into their false beliefs and begin to feel a bit more comfortable and self-confident, the group provides a setting within which they can practice alternative types of behavior. Role playing is very useful at this point because it provides practice in what to say and how to act in initiating contact with others. More specifics about using role plays will be discussed in Chapter 4. Suffice it to say that generally, once group members receive a positive response, their self-confidence increases and they begin to relax enough so that a conversation can flow. Creating sufficient cognitive dissonance about these false self-beliefs so that the restructuring process can begin is the most difficult step.

PRACTICING NEW BEHAVIORS

The next step is for members to try the new behavior outside the group in situations that they have imagined and discussed. Members are asked to report back to the group on how the interaction went and how they felt at the time. This process serves several purposes: Members share their experiences, try new behaviors, are encouraged to talk about their feelings, and receive support and reassurance even when the attempts are not successful. They receive encouragement to try again, and alternative behaviors are suggested and practiced. Even a terrible "failure" can have a very positive ending when the individual receives empathy, support, and positive affirmations of his or her character from group members who freely express their caring and concern.

❑ Summary

As is readily apparent, the goals, just like the issues that they seek to address, are interrelated, and achievement of one is contingent upon progress made toward another. Breaking through the isolation that members feel and providing them with a supportive, consistent environment are critical to creating an atmosphere where problems can be examined, feelings expressed, and interpersonal skills learned. Progress toward achievement of specific goals varies across group sessions depending upon which issues become more or less pressing.

The pursuit of goals is often as therapeutic and helpful as the actual attainment because many of these adults have never really defined or set goals for their personal or interpersonal lives. Besides the resistance that can be expected, adult survivors manifest untiring enthusiasm and desire to overcome their pasts and make their future lives happier and more satisfying.

The goals for growth that individual group members have are, we believe, best achieved within a group setting. The next chapter will examine the advantages of group treatment and also point out the special complications that can arise when working with survivors of child abuse.

3

Advantages and Challenges
of Using the Group Process

"I'm not the only one! I can't tell you what a relief it is to discover that. For so long I have been so ashamed. I thought I was the only person bad enough to be treated like this."

—29-year-old male group member

"I can't believe you all believe me. When I asked my pastor for help when I was a teenager, he didn't believe me—my father was a member of the church council. For a while I wasn't sure I believed myself."

—34-year-old female group member

"You mean it's all right to ask for help? Whenever I did that at home I was either laughed at or ignored. Sometimes my mother would hit me and call me stupid. It's really difficult for me to admit I need anything."

—32-year-old female group member

As we noted in the preface, a major reason for attempting a group approach to treatment for adult survivors was to break the circle of isolation that developed as a result of their abusive experiences. Those who have participated in the support groups, even though they initially joined with a certain uneasy eagerness, have identified the breaking down of isolation as a major advantage for them. The opportunity to finally disrupt a lifelong pattern of hiding a supposedly embarrassing fact produced a great sense of relief. Members of these groups have been remarkably faithful to the group for long periods of time and have exhibited surprising levels of trust in sharing about their abuse, especially in view of learned patterns of avoiding self-disclosure.

❏ Advantages of Group Treatment

VALIDATION

Although the common bond that the members experience is an important aspect of the group process for adult survivors, several other advantages to the group approach soon become evident. A principal advantage is the validation, or affirmation, of one's reality that occurs in the group. Yalom (1985) has identified validation as a common advantage to group treatment. It is especially powerful for survivors of child abuse (Agosta & Loring, 1988; Courtois, 1988; Herman, 1992; Sprei, 1986; van der Kolk, 1987; Vannicelli, 1989). The simple fact is that when persons with similar abusive backgrounds gather together to share their experiences, they achieve a realization about the similarity of their experience that they cannot acquire by reading books about child abuse. They experience what Judith Herman (1992) calls the "euphoria of finding one another" (p. 224).

A male group member once exemplified this very poignantly. Properly dressed in a gray business suit, he sat quietly as several group members introduced themselves and made statements about the abuse in their past. When his turn came, tears welled in his eyes and he said,

I'm ashamed to say this, but I'm very glad to hear what people have been saying. I don't mean that I am happy about what happened to you or about the difficulties you are experiencing, but I can't tell you what a relief it is to know I'm not the only one this kind of thing happened to, and I'm not the only one having some of the problems you all have mentioned. And you all seem quite nice. Maybe there's some hope for me after all.

The statistics about the pervasiveness of abuse in our society become real, and group members finally feel that they are not the only people to whom this has happened. They are living proof of the statistics. They find solace in the similarities of their experiences, and they begin to sense that they are not as evil as they had believed because the same things have happened to someone else who seems to be a good person.

Their feelings are also validated and affirmed. As they see the grief and sadness of others, their own pain becomes more legitimate, and they can acknowledge and own it. When they realize that others also are frustrated or anxious, they can confront those feelings in themselves with a new, less self-deprecating perspective. As they experience anger at what was done to others, they can admit their own anger at what was done to them.

This experience of validation also enables group members to be accepting of one another. Because of their common backgrounds, they are able to listen to one another without the reactions of horror or disbelief with which friends and even counselors frequently greet their accounts. No one in the group will dispute the reality of the experience or be so shocked as to be unable to offer comfort. Even the most gruesome accounts are listened to with nods of understanding and acceptance. Instead of having to prove, defend, or interpret the experience, the former victim can move directly to confronting the present personal problems that have resulted from it.

This experience of a common reality has an important impact on the first meeting of any group. Although the first session understandably begins with a lot of hesitation and nervousness, after the first brave member shares something of his or her abusive background, others, with a great sense of relief, quickly follow suit. The depth of sharing, of course, varies from person to person, but once the process has started, no one has ever failed to acknowledge some aspect of the experience that he or she had never discussed with anyone before.

Many new group leaders approach their first meeting with a great deal of concern. They wonder how they will get the group to start and whether there will be enough material to keep the meeting going for 2 hours. Once the leaders introduce the purpose of the group and reiterate the fact that former abuse experiences are the one thing that everyone has in common, all it takes is one person brave enough to start the process. The only problem thereafter is controlling individual revelations so that everyone has a chance to speak during the 2 hours.

Repeatedly, new leaders report their amazement at the amount and depth of sharing that takes place in the first meeting. This, we believe, is a product of the experience of feeling affirmed and validated. No group process technique can encourage sharing as much as the assurance that one is going to be fully understood, accepted, and affirmed.

This validating, or empathic legitimizing of one's experiences and feelings, also has a strong effect as the group moves beyond the point of sharing past experiences and starts dealing with present problems (usually by the third session). We have found that group members are more able to acknowledge the value of help offered when it comes from others with a similar history. The same is true of challenges for change. When suggestions for how to resolve a problem or questions about the effectiveness of modes of behavior come from a group of people that has had similar experiences, they have greater impact. Comments like the following are frequently heard: "Maybe that suggestion can really work since it comes from someone like you who knows what I have experienced." "Maybe I can accomplish that change since you have gone through the same things I have and you have done it."

Over and over again, pressure or encouragement from other group members has moved a member to action when the repeated urging of a group leader has apparently fallen on deaf ears. The same words of encouragement, the same suggested solutions or approaches to a problem suddenly have a different significance, are finally heard, or heard in a new way, and are applied when they come from a group member who has struggled with the same difficulty. Repeatedly, leaders find that solutions or encouragement offered to no avail 2 weeks earlier, when repeated (not half so eloquently) by a group member, are acclaimed as the greatest wisdom since the death of Solomon. It may be that the member is ready to hear the advice by the second time it is offered, but it also may be that members can take it better from others with similar experiences.

The recognition of success also can be more real within a group of peers. Their beliefs about themselves start to change. Now they can believe: "Maybe that accomplishment is significant, if the members of my group think it is"; "At last, someone recognizes how difficult it is to accomplish that one little task."

Finally, we have found that the validation process has a feedback loop effect on participants. As one group member helps another achieve some new insight, that same understanding may have personal meaning to the originator of the idea. For example: "I just told him that he couldn't be responsible for what happened because he was only six years old when it happened. I was only five when a similar thing happened to me." Time and time again, group members have stopped in the middle of an eloquent dissertation on a recommended behavior or attitude change for someone else. With a sheepish grin, they mumble: "I guess I should really follow my own advice."

The process often works as a positive form of catch-22. Members catch each other with their own advice. "You are now telling me the same thing the whole group has been telling you for weeks. Let's make a deal. If you will follow your own advice, I will try to do the same. We can report at the next meeting how it went."

The group can also validate the pain, sadness, and grief that survivors quite rightly feel about their family of origin. They often feel angry and cheated by the kind of family life they experienced. To have others express similar emotions allows them to acknowledge such feelings and know they are not alone in the group.

SAFE ENVIRONMENT

There are other major advantages of a group approach to treatment for survivors that should be highlighted here. The first such advantage is that it provides them with the safe, supportive environment that most of them have never experienced. By "safe," we mean a place where they can feel free to talk about any thought, feeling, or belief without fear of being accused, attacked (verbally or physically), criticized, ridiculed, or disparaged. In many ways, the group provides the kind of family or community experience that the former abuse victim has always sought.

The safe, supportive atmosphere fosters opportunities for the individual to experiment with and learn new behaviors without fear of retaliation. Old beliefs can be analyzed, and the skills developed for survival in the home environment can be reevaluated for their appropriateness in the rest of the society. Interactions within this new, supportive environment can help foster new, positive images of oneself. Members learn that they can ask for support and assistance openly and honestly rather than resort to manipulation or passivity.

One example that illustrates the effect of a supportive environment involves a very soft-spoken member of a group.

> Because he was so quiet and soft-spoken, Ed was frequently asked by other members to speak louder and repeat himself. This often seemed to upset him and cause him to withdraw. When questioned about the behavior, he became angry and accused the group of being just like his parents, who always ridiculed the way he talked and made fun of him for not talking. The group pointed out that they were not ridiculing—they really wanted to hear what he had to say. For them to do that, he had to speak louder.
>
> Ed finally admitted that he had not spoken until he was 4 years old. His family frequently derided him for this; therefore, any comment about his speech was associated with his family. After some discussion, Ed was able to realize that other people could ask him to speak up and not be mocking him.

The group then became for Ed what his family had never been: a supportive community that encouraged him to express himself and develop his ideas. By understanding and using the negative transference in this situation, Ed was able to "reframe" his beliefs about what was happening when people asked him to speak louder. He could begin to see their prompting as a positive expression of interest in him. He now had a place where he could feel comfortable speaking.

OPPORTUNITIES FOR PRACTICE

This example brings us to the second advantage of using a group approach to treatment: opportunities for practice. The group setting provides a multidimensional arena for the former victim to practice interpersonal communication and other life skills. Participation in group discussions and problem-solving efforts naturally provides experience in the dialogue and give-and-take involved in normal conversational opportunities that members' family lives failed to provide. The members also learn to express their views before at least a small group of people—a new and important step for most of them.

Frequently, members use the group as an opportunity to do a "practice run" on a presentation they are going to make or a discussion they plan to have with a friend or family member. As they become increasingly comfortable, members request time to talk about the content of their proposed discussion or to role-play it. Sometimes, they simply ask the group for some words of support and encouragement before they embark on what would be a very ordinary discussion for most people.

Disclosure of personal information and feelings can be practiced in the group settings. This broadens the private testimony about abuse that may have occurred during individual therapy, giving it a "judicial, public aspect" (Herman, 1992, p. 221) that gives the survivor a new sense of power and control. Members can also discuss and explore boundary setting. In the group setting, they learn to distinguish and respect others' boundaries and to see that boundaries differ from individual to individual and in various situations. For example, related to contact with each other outside the group, members are encouraged to set any limits or restrictions, such as how late or how frequently or where (i.e., home, workplace) they may be contacted.

Finally, effective problem solving and decision making can be learned and practiced in the safe, supportive environment of the group. Members can identify, practice, and use different problem-solving techniques and can support one another in managing life problems and making decisions. When they see that there is a strategy that can be learned and mastered or a plan that can be developed and followed, the "magic" is removed from taking control of their lives.

ROLE MODELING

Yalom (1985) speaks of the "installation of hope" (p. 6) as a primary therapeutic factor of therapy groups. This occurs as members who are at various stages of healing or recovery observe others' improvement and feel increased optimism about their own chances for change and success. For example, it was especially reassuring for a new group member who was painfully shy and very uncomfortable speaking in the group to hear an experienced group member talk about her anxiety and embarrassment at not being able to "even open her mouth to tell her name" at the first meeting she attended. The shy woman responded with surprise and disbelief, "I can't believe that you were ever shy. You're so relaxed and self-confident. If I get half as good as you, I'll be happy."

There is also the possibility in a group of having a variety of role models. Group members can imitate one another's successful behavioral and cognitive changes. They can observe which strategies work in various situations and can be emulated as well as those that are not as successful and should be avoided. Furthermore, they have the advantage of being able to observe different individual coping styles. They learn that there can be many options from which to choose.

INFORMATION SHARING

Another important function of the group that is especially helpful to adult survivors is the sharing and discussing of information about daily living. Like adult children of alcoholics who "don't know what normal is," survivors of child abuse also have a skewed or distorted perception of what are "correct," appropriate, or acceptable thoughts, behaviors, and feelings. The group provides an arena in which to question, discuss, and debate everything from how to do grocery shopping and organize their living space to what is appropriate behavior in a friendship or intimate relationship. For many survivors, the group is the only safe place to ask these "embarrassing" questions because they believe they should already know the answers. If "shame is a response to helplessness" (Herman, 1992, p. 53), and information is power, as computer-age doctrine tells us, then the information-sharing function of group therapy will not only facilitate powerful cognitive and behavioral changes but also promote growth in self-esteem and emotional healing.

GIVING BACK

A final benefit of group therapy is what Yalom (1985) calls the "altruism" factor of the group. We call this the opportunity to "give something back." In the group, individuals not only receive nurturance and support, they also care for and help one another. This fosters self-esteem at the same time that it teaches healthy patterns for giving support. When one member tells another, "What you said to me last meeting was really helpful," or "The fact that you called last night to encourage me before I took my test gave me the boost I needed to do well," individuals begin to realize that they are worthwhile and have something to offer others—something they didn't hear at home. This experience of "giving back" also enhances group members' self-respect and self-confidence in other social relationships as they are able to extend this behavior beyond the group (Jehu, 1988). Because of their experiences in a group, members are often inspired and empowered to speak out privately to friends or publicly in classes and small groups about the effects of child abuse, or even participate in or lead public rallies denouncing abuse. Some have even volunteered to share their experiences on radio or television talk shows. They see these public education opportunities as ways that they can exert some control over the violence of the world. This new sense of power is extremely therapeutic.

❏ Complications in Group Treatment

Despite these advantages of group treatment for adult survivors of child abuse (and they are significant), there are complications that can arise as a result of the dynamics created by abuse. These complications, which can have a critical impact on the success of the group process, arise because former abuse victims do not react in a group setting in the same way as people without a history of abuse. Former victims have learned some distinctive survival patterns and defense mechanisms; these constitute survival skills that were essential and highly adaptive in the dysfunctional family settings. However, these patterns and mechanisms are maladaptive outside of that setting and can short-circuit the effective workings not only of group process but also of daily living and communication. Group leaders must be aware of these distinctive characteristics so that they can move the group beyond potential breakdown to individual and group healing. These factors will be examined in this section.

DISTORTED COMMUNICATION

As we have noted, the communication patterns of former victims often have been distorted by the abusive environment in which the victims lived. They learned at an early age to hide, mask, and even deny feelings and needs. Although the group members are no longer in their family setting, the negative messages and instinctive defense reactions learned there are still very much a part of their lives.

All too frequently, survivors view relationships with others from the perspective of fear, anxious watchfulness, and shame. Their expectation is that others will hurt, ridicule, or take advantage of them. Survivors have learned to get what they want by manipulation rather than forthright communication. Their parents so often ignored their needs, refused to respond to their requests, or blatantly thwarted their efforts to take care of themselves that artifice and craftiness are their primary tools for self-care.

For many survivors, ordinary, present-day events remind them of past abuse. These events trigger responses conditioned by the abuse rather than the present reality. Therefore, they respond with fear or suspicion to words and gestures intended to be caring and supportive. Because they heard so many negative comments from their parents, they assume every remark directed to them is negative or a rejection. When they do encounter someone who is abusive to them as adults (such as bosses, store clerks, and cab drivers), they react as a frightened child rather than as a competent adult.

Even if the members know intellectually that they should react differently in the present setting, their instinctive reaction is to fall back on previous behavior patterns. As with the example of soft-spoken Ed, they know that they are not dealing with their parents and that they are free in the group to express their feelings, but that does not come easily or naturally. Their instinctive response is to withdraw or to deny their own emotions.

This is especially true when anger is expressed, disagreements arise, or criticism is offered. These instinctive protective patterns immediately reappear. Members become fearful and withdrawn. Discussions come to a frightened halt. Such experiences are distressingly similar to the situations that triggered violent episodes in their families. They are not fully able to distinguish the circumstances.

PASSIVE-AGGRESSIVE COMMUNICATION

Passive-aggressive methods of communication are also common in these groups. It is difficult to elicit clear statements of needs and desires. Members prefer not to state their wishes rather than to make a request that may be ignored, rejected, or ridiculed. Particular members often complain that the leaders or the group members are not paying enough attention to them, but this comes only after long periods of silence or minimal participation. It is only after special efforts are made to draw a person out that the group member complains that he or she has felt ignored. At other times, members request help at the very end of a meeting when there is not adequate time to deal with the issue.

> Joan was particularly adept at this distortion of communication. Many times, she would sit quietly through a whole meeting; then, as time was running out, she would bring up an important issue. Because of previous commitments, people had to leave and the topic would be postponed.
>
> At the next meeting, she would be asked at the very beginning to introduce her concern again. Responses were varied: Sometimes, she would respond with anger, saying that it was now too late to do

anything about it; other times, she would simply say that the issue was no longer important and that it was not necessary to talk about it anymore.

The leaders and group members found this very frustrating and tried several methods to deal with this recurring problem. They tried to anticipate the problem by asking Joan early in sessions to state any concerns she might have. Often, she would say she had nothing important and then proceed to drop another "bomb" at the end of the meeting. Other times, she would ask to wait until later, saying that it took her a while to feel comfortable enough to share. This necessitated frequent "checking back" to see if she was ready. At some meetings, she would finally state her concerns in time to deal with them; other times, she would not.

The group also held long, rational discussions with Joan about why people had to leave at the time appointed for the end of meetings and why concerns needed to be brought up earlier. Some of the discussions also focused on the self-defeating nature of Joan's communication process and why she needed to overcome her fear of sharing and hasten the time when she felt comfortable. Group members assured her over and over again that they really did want to discuss her concerns and that they would take them seriously if they were given enough time to do so. They pointed out that her habit of waiting until it was too late to deal with the issue may have worked as a defense with her family, because by not giving them enough time to discuss the issue she also did not give them time to ridicule and reject her. They emphasized that she did not need that defense with the group.

On occasion, the discussions got emotional as group members became increasingly frustrated whenever Joan would "do it to them again." They clearly recognized the manipulative nature of Joan's process and became tired of the controlling nature of this process and the "guilt trip" it worked on them.

No single event or discussion ever completely reformed Joan's behavior. She did gradually become more open and forthright about her needs and concerns. On occasion, she would even state early in a meeting, "I have something I need to talk about. Will you help me talk about it?" But the process was always slow and painful. It often seemed that the group spent more time talking about why something should be discussed than actually talking about the issue. Nevertheless, Joan did learn to state some of her needs and ask for help with her problems.

Although Joan may have taken more time than most people to learn to discuss her concerns, the resistance she exhibited is not uncommon. Most survivors experience great fear and anxiety when sharing their feelings. Therefore, gentle encouragement is very important as group members make their first tentative attempts to share their feelings and experiences. Great sensitivity and much assistance with understanding, expression, and interpretation are necessary as members get back in touch with their own needs, learn to state them, and seek their fulfillment.

TRAUMA-RELATED RESPONSES

When communication finally does begin to take place, it may have other effects on the group process. Most frequently, it is an informing and liberating experience for other members. Sometimes, however, one person's sharing of a past experience may trigger recollections or even flashbacks of blocked experiences for another person.

Such flashbacks can be very powerful and disconcerting for someone who has successfully denied the experience for many years. Therefore, group leaders must be constantly vigilant about what is happening to all the members of the group. They must be alert enough to recognize the symptoms of the flashback process and sensitive enough to provide understanding and support. This will be discussed further in Chapter 4. These experiences, of course, create yet another disruption in the process of the group's life.

HYPERSENSITIVITY AS A DEFENSE MECHANISM

Despite communication problems, one of the most distinctive features of adult survivor groups is that the initial formation process generally moves quickly and smoothly. The membership, of course, is self-selected, and once the participants have identified themselves as former victims and overcome their initial anxiety about participating in such a group, they are eager to get on with the task. As we have noted, the members experience a great deal of relief at finally being able to share their abusive experiences and being understood.

This opportunity to break out of their isolation and share with people with similar experiences creates a profound sense of belonging that many have never experienced before. The group becomes an oasis in their lives. This sense of community creates a strong bond of loyalty that is further enhanced by the fact that the group members also exhibit an unusually high level of perceptual sensitivity and an ability to understand the feelings and emotions of the other members of the group. Therefore, group formation and bonding process are accomplished very quickly.

This is an accurate description of the initial meetings of a survivors' group. The group members are very sincere about the importance of the group for them and about their concern for one another. However, because of the dynamics of abuse, these initial experiences are deceptive. This high level of sensitivity and understanding is motivated by the same fear and mistrust that has ruled their lives for so long. Adult survivors use this sensitivity (or hypersensitivity) to *protect and defend* themselves against others, *not* as a tool to deepen a relationship. Although a certain amount of defensiveness is prevalent, and may even be proper in our society, the defensiveness of survivors extends far beyond what is normal and appropriate. It influences all their interpersonal relationships and their behaviors. Fear and distrust even influence their interpersonal sensitivity.

The former abuse victim's ability to be sensitive to the moods and emotions of others is highly developed. In fact, it operates at a level that makes those of us who have worked with these groups envious. They seem to read the feelings of other group members and the leaders as soon as they walk in the door, as illustrated by the following example.

> On one occasion while we were processing the previous group session, my coleader confessed that she had a particularly bad day before the previous meeting. She wondered whether I had been aware of it and whether I thought the group members had noticed any changes in her behavior. I acknowledged being vaguely conscious of her tension but assured her that the group would not have observed it. It was not that evident.
>
> To the surprise of both of us, that was the first item the group members brought up at the next meeting. Some of them had met for coffee in the intervening week (the pros and cons of such contacts have been discussed in Chapter 2) and had shared the fact that they feared that one of the leaders might have been upset with them. They were relieved to discover that the feeling was mutual; therefore, not directed at any of them personally. Reinforced by their mutual perception, they were emboldened to raise it in the meeting.

The coleader immediately acknowledged that events earlier on that day had upset and preoccupied her. They were the reasons for her mood at the previous meeting. The ensuing discussion revealed the acuteness of the group members' powers of observation. They easily identified several telltale behaviors that had been clues to my coleader's tension. I had missed many of them.

This incident highlights the acuity and sensitivity of the perceptions of former abuse victims. What we must remember is that this praiseworthy and finely tuned skill was developed for protective purposes, and that is the motivation that continues to drive it. During childhood, this ability to recognize the moods of their parents was an essential survival skill. To avoid abuse, they had to be constantly alert to how their abusive parent might be feeling. Thus, the interpersonal sensitivity exhibited by the group members is really an unconscious, automatic defense mechanism rather than a tool for establishing interpersonal contact and intimacy.

Group members generally are not aware that they are avoiding intimate relationships. Nevertheless, the defensive character of their sensitivity hampers their ability to respond to the very feelings they identify. When any unpleasant feelings (anger, sorrow) are recognized, the process of communication comes to a sudden halt. Causes are not explored, motives are not discussed, and methods for resolution are not considered. No method for dealing with these feelings, other than withdrawal, is considered possible. This, of course, impedes the effectiveness of the group bonding process. Despite the early sense of community cohesion, the underlying fear continues to paralyze members as they attempt to capitalize on the bond they have developed. Even their best intentions are sometimes thwarted by their inbred mistrust. Members must be encouraged and assisted to use their interpersonal sensitivity as a tool for exploring relationships with others.

This hypervigilance and hypersensitivity to the moods and wishes of others also can have a negative impact on the self-revelation process of members of the group. Their abusive experience taught them to be keenly aware of and responsive to even the unspoken expectations of the people around them. Their preoccupation with the need to recognize and respond to the preferences and needs of others as a means of self-protection not only makes it difficult for them to reveal their own needs and preferences, but it also makes it difficult for them to even identify their own expectations. Their family experience taught them that it was essential for self-preservation to focus on the needs and expectations of others. This strengthens their ability to be helpful, supportive, and nurturing to others in the group, but they find it difficult to identify and meet their own needs.

If, as children, they did learn to recognize their own needs and to state them to their parents, they often experienced denial, ridicule, rejection, or punishment. They were made to feel guilty for such selfishness, or they found their needs being taken advantage of sexually or emotionally. Soon, such desires were not even allowed to reach the conscious level. The guilt and fear were too painful.

These responses continue into adulthood. Over and over again, it has happened that when group members finally allow personal needs to break through and be acknowledged, they suddenly stop themselves short. They immediately ask, "Is it all right for me to want this?" "Isn't it wrong to ask for this?" "Are you sure this is OK?" They cannot believe that they are entitled to commonly accepted forms of care and nurturance. They fear that their needs will become vehicles for abuse once again. They find it hard to accept that they have a right not only to have certain feelings but also to have their needs fulfilled. Too often, their feelings and desires have been taken advantage of, rejected, or punished.

Because of these experiences and their resultant effect on present behaviors, the self-revelation process in the group context is short circuited at many different points. This breakdown in the flow of information about needs and expectations within the group negatively influences the group's ability to provide meaningful acceptance to members and for the members to feel accepted. When individuals do not fully reveal their personal needs and desires, others cannot take those factors into account in dealing with them. These individuals then quite naturally, but unintentionally, feel that they are not fully accepted by the group. All of this makes realistic and meaningful group bonding difficult both for individual members and for the group as a whole. Group leaders must constantly be tuned in to unspoken needs and encourage and reinforce self-disclosure by group members.

LEARNING TO BELIEVE THAT ONE IS ACCEPTABLE

As we discussed previously, adult survivors of abuse have very low self-esteem and a profound sense of personal inadequacy. This quite naturally affects their ability to believe that others truly accept and care for them. Despite the affinity that exists between group members and the sense of belonging that evolves from their common past, these survivors still have difficulty being convinced that others accept them. This disbelief can interfere with group participation and even result in fear of rejection.

This reluctance to believe they are accepted and acceptable has two sources. The first, discussed above, is that because of their inability to clearly identify and express their own goals, aspirations, and needs, they never feel understood. Second, they have learned and retain an ingrained conviction that they are worthless and unlovable. Constant expressions of reassurance are necessary from the leaders as well as the members of the group.

As any member shares a past experience or a past or present feeling (whether unpleasant or positive) with the group, it is important to take time to reaffirm that member's continuing acceptance by the other members. In their families, the expression of unacceptable feelings (which could be anything someone in the family disagreed with or found uncomfortable) often produced abuse. Also, the sharing of abuse experiences with friends frequently triggered avoidance because of horror or disbelief. That expectation of rejection carries over even into a group formed specifically for people with similar abuse experiences.

The fear of not being accepted may manifest itself at various times during the life of a group especially whenever new, particularly difficult information is shared. Even though members feel accepted by their peers and the group leaders, they often feel certain that a new revelation may destroy their acceptance by the group. On more than one occasion, members who have attended a group regularly for several months suddenly miss several meetings in a row. Inquiries reveal that they stopped coming because they were embarrassed for having made some new disclosure and were sure the group would not want them back. The expectation of rejection is deeply ingrained.

The group members' expectations of rejection also create much suspicion and concern about motives and consistency. Everyone in the group is subject to testing and evaluation, but most especially group leaders because of their authority position (Courtois, 1988). The persistent fear, even expectation, is that the leaders, like their parents, will find something wrong with them and will punish or reject them. Group members constantly watch the group leaders for signs of approval or disapproval. Over and over again, group members turn to the leaders to receive assurance and affirmation for what they say or do.

Even when such approval is given, its sincerity and constancy may be doubted. Many times, we have found members resurrecting issues and concerns that we thought had been dealt with and resolved weeks before. They return to the topic to make sure we still approve of their action and have not changed our minds. The resurrection of former topics often is not done directly but slipped into the middle of some other discussion with some slight variation on the original theme. It almost seems that the attempt is to see whether, if the question is asked in a slightly different way, a different answer will be forthcoming. Therefore, they need to be constantly reassured.

Second, even if their actions were sanctioned by their family, the continuance of such approval was not guaranteed. What was encouraged at one moment might be ridiculed at another time. Therefore, they need to frequently check back to see if the approval continues. For them, it often seems an issue is never completely resolved.

This inconsistency of parental response also has an impact on the development of survivor groups. As described in Chapter 2, one of the goals for groups is to establish a consistent, predictable, and structured environment. Although this goal is intended to foster the development of trust and promote growth and healing, it is the antithesis of the chaos and unpredictability that are often the standard modes of operating in abusive homes. It challenges the comfort with chaos that we identified in Chapter 1 as part of the dynamic for abuse survivors. Thus, complications related to consistency versus chaos arise in the group.

Because chaos seems more natural to them, group members may find it extremely difficult to identify and accept roles for themselves in a group. They may be uncomfortable concentrating attention on any one topic or person, or being the focus of the group. They may find it difficult to concentrate on a particular topic until it is concluded.

All too frequently, they will change the subject very deftly before anything is settled. They do this either to get the pressure off of themselves when they are being pushed to make a decision or to rescue someone else from such pressure. Because of their past experience, they fear that such pressure may turn hostile, or that even if a decision or resolution is reached, it will be considered wrong by someone and therefore result in verbal or physical abuse. They think the best course of action is to change the subject before the discussion reaches either of those two possibilities. Therefore, they are much more at ease with dispersed and frequently shifting attention. They are more comfortable with chaos than with structure, order, and focus.

Group leaders must frequently intervene to point out that a topic has not been concluded or a decision has not been reached and gently but firmly refocus the discussion. Even though group members may initially complain about the rigid structure of the group, they gradually come to appreciate its importance. They soon realize that only by experiencing conclusions and making decisions that are affirmed rather than ridiculed will they learn that they can, in fact, make good decisions.

The past chaos of their family life makes control of their environment seem impossible for many adult survivors. They were never able to easily influence their environment; therefore, they learned early to develop passive-aggressive means of control, communication, and conflict avoidance. The means of manipulation range from silence and withdrawal, to incessant talking about unconnected issues, to frequent changes in discussion topics. To counteract these problems resulting from the group members' chaotic pasts, it is important, especially in the early stages of the group, to have a fairly rigid structure and process. This serves as a learning experience so that group members can begin to feel comfortable in a controlled and controllable environment. It also ensures that each person gets adequate "air time," topics are adhered to, issues are brought to conclusion, and tasks get accomplished. All of these are important experiences for group members, who need to develop a sense of control over their environment, which in turn provides a sense of accomplishment and self-esteem.

PROBLEMS WITH GOAL SETTING

Despite these difficulties, the group does form, esprit de corps develops, members establish relationships, and communication does take place. The group members do get down to the business of defining roles and establishing personal and group goals. However, even in this goal-setting process, the effects of growing up in an abusive family are readily apparent.

Members often have difficulty establishing meaningful and real-istic goals for themselves or for the group. This problem manifests itself in different ways. Some survivors may be evasive about deter-mining anything specific; others may tend to set idealistic and unattainable goals. We believe that dynamics from their abusive pasts contribute to these problems with goal setting.

Most children in abusive homes had little or no control over their environment. The abuse they experienced robbed them of a sense of power over what did or did not happen to them. Often, they were never sure from one moment to the next whether or not plans they made could be carried out. Goals they set were frequently sabo-taged.

Also, as we discussed in Chapter 1, children in abusive environ-ments were taught little about proper goal setting, or they learned that it was a "no-win" task. Their parents either did not know how to do it themselves, so they could not offer training and guidance, or they simply ignored their children and left them to their own devices, or they punished the children no matter what goals they set or decisions they made.

Regardless of which scenario played out in their family experi-ence, for many survivors, goal setting is a painful process. It is not something that ever provided them with any meaningful sense of accomplishment. They often did not know whether they had succeeded or failed. No matter how successful or conscientious they were, it was never good enough.

Thus, survivors may have problems with goal setting for various reasons. They simply may not know how to analyze a situation and choose between options or alternatives. They also may have internalized unrealistic expectations for themselves and continue to set unattainable goals. They may fear setting goals because they are convinced that they cannot fulfill them. They were never able to do so to their parents' satisfaction. They were frequently criticized, ridiculed, or physically abused for their failure to attain their parents' goals. These people have negative associations with goal setting. They believe that goal setting has many negative consequences and few, if any, positive results.

Whatever the source of the problems with goal setting, this part of the group's process is extremely important. It is necessary for any group to function effectively, but for this clientele, it has a practical therapeutic role. By practicing goal setting in the group, the members can learn to set reasonable (i.e., realistic and attainable) and measurable (i.e., so individuals can chart their progress) goals for their lives.

The "reasonable and measurable" aspect of the previous statement is also extremely difficult for former victims. Once the fear and anxiety are overcome (and that may have to be done repeatedly, each time new goals are established), much work must be done to ensure that the goals set are realistic and meaningful.

This problem, of course, stems from a lack of experience. With so little background to draw from, survivors have no effective measure of what is attainable. Some will set extremely high goals; others set very low goals. This is often a result of their lack of knowledge about what is realistic on either the high or the low end of the scale. Some, however, set their goals very high in an attempt to please the group leaders and as a way to get the praise and acceptance they never got as children. Others set their goals very low because of their low self-esteem and as an attempt to avoid failure.

The members of both categories must be helped to find a realistic middle ground and then to break down the goal attainment process into manageable steps. All too often, group members do not understand that most tasks have several intermediate steps. They attempt to get from Point A to Point Z without realizing that there may be 24 steps in between. Again, this may stem from their simple lack of experience; however, some of it also arises from their obsessive need to be perfect in order to finally get some approval. To take too long is a sign of weakness or imperfection, and they will not get the acceptance they so desperately crave.

When members do set goals (e.g. to make new friends, be more assertive, talk with others about their abuse) and begin to make changes and to grow, they frequently find themselves uneasy and uncomfortable with the changes. During this period, their dependence on the group may increase, and they will credit any improvements in their condition to the group as a whole or to the leaders in particular. This too is a product of their abusive experience. They do not have enough self-esteem to give themselves any credit. This also is a defensive move. If they give the credit for achievements to the group or leader, they can also pass on the blame in case they regress or fail at a later time. All accomplishments need to be acknowledged in the group by all members, and individuals must be given credit for what they have attained.

SAFETY IN SIMILARITY

Feelings of low self-esteem also can influence the creation of alliances or relationships within the group, and often they prove counterproductive. For example, some members may feel affinity for one another because of what they perceive as similar levels of coping. Sometimes, we hear one member say to another, "I know just what you're feeling. I know what you're going through and that it is very difficult. You and I have a lot in common." This kind of statement is very reassuring and supportive for the one to whom it is addressed, and we encourage such empathic responses between members.

However, sometimes this kind of response can be counterproductive. Although such reassurance is essential if former victims are going to be freed of the sense of isolation and guilt that stems from their abusive experiences, it must not be allowed to become the basis for continuing inappropriate behaviors or as an excuse for not making necessary changes. It can happen that the participants in such an alliance are so relieved to find someone struggling with the same problem that the pressure for growth or resolution is diminished. They seem to think, "If he (or she) has a similar difficulty, maybe it's okay to be this way."

The desire for safety in similarity often dictates this sense of identification and alliance. Both of the people involved are familiar with their present patterns of behavior, and because they have now found someone else who identifies with those same patterns, they can continue their present coping strategies without feeling isolated and bizarre.

Even if that dynamic does not influence the relationship between the two parties, another set of problems can arise when one of the people begins to make changes. No matter which of the two people initiates a change in his or her life, the other person may feel betrayed and abandoned, and, in fact, may react negatively to the person who is changing. Accusations and put-downs are not uncommon as the "abandoned" partner acts out his or her frustration and even attempts to keep the other party at the same level of coping.

> On one occasion, we had two people in the same group who were very quiet. Even though they did not say much to each other, there was an immediate affinity; they felt comfortable with one another. After participating in the group for several weeks and achieving a level of personal comfort with the group, Linda decided that one of her goals in the group was to become more assertive. She began to speak more freely and ask for time to share her concerns.
>
> As Linda became more and more active in the group, her "friend," Ellen, became even more quiet. Ellen's withdrawal became especially evident on occasions when Linda was talking about her concerns. On one occasion, Linda shared that Ellen had snubbed her when they met one another outside the group. The group confronted Ellen and encouraged her to share what was troubling her. She began by attacking Linda, "You don't like me anymore. You never pay any attention to me. I used to feel close to you, but I don't anymore. I don't even know you anymore. I can't relate to you."
>
> With the help of the group, Linda was able to respond positively to Ellen's charges. She pointed out that she was not rejecting Ellen and still felt a strong kinship with her, but that she was also trying to accomplish one of her goals for joining the group. She hoped that Ellen would accept her as she continued to grow and that Ellen would

also consider trying to be more assertive because Linda had found it a very positive experience.

Actually, Ellen did begin to make her own changes, but she and Linda never reestablished their old, natural affinity. The stereotypes within which they had established their original relationship were no longer operational. Their association now had to be based on factors more realistic and complex than their quiet natures.

Occasionally, such a stereotyping process takes place within the group as a whole. One member is perceived as the quiet one, another as the talker, still another as the vulnerable member who must be protected, and yet another as the strong member who "has it more together" and does not need the same care as the other members of the group. These roles are sometimes imposed by the other members of the group, but often are self-imposed by the individuals themselves. They learned these roles in their families, often as defense mechanisms, and continue to act them out in any group setting.

Many times, the group roles assumed by members are continuations of their roles in their families, and they begin to exhibit the defensive survival skills they learned. These roles include the family caretaker or scapegoat; the passive, helpless victim who needs to be protected; the aggressive, hostile family protector; the compliant "good child"; or the provocateur. Group leaders must continually monitor the roles that members assume and offer encouragement and support as members experiment with new behaviors and ways of interacting.

DISTORTION OF FEEDBACK

The use of feedback is probably the most difficult element of group interaction for an adult survivors' group to implement. Sharing reactions to other members, seeking clarification about others' comments, and feeling free to confront and criticize one another are difficult for people in most groups (Yalom, 1985). However, these problems are greatly magnified in survivors' groups. This magnification stems from three factors. As we have discussed, abuse survivors are accustomed to receiving primarily destructive and derogatory feedback. Therefore, they find it difficult to hear positive, laudatory comments, even when they are offered. Positive remarks may not be heard at all or may be interpreted as negative.

If the feedback offered is at all critical, recipients hear it as insulting and demeaning. No matter how positively and gently observations are phrased, the group members perceive a put-down and immediately become defensive. This is again consistent with their previous experience. Much of the feedback they received as children was negative and demeaning, a sign that someone did not like them. Many comments about their behaviors were expressed as criticisms of them as people. They were called bad, evil children, not just children who had done something wrong. Therefore, it is now difficult for them to distinguish between criticism of their actions and criticism of themselves as people.

The final factor is that for former abuse victims, critical feedback did not stop at demeaning remarks; it often resulted in physical violence. They recall that such comments frequently were the prelude to violence. Therefore, that is their present expectation.

Given the final two factors, it is understandable that survivors react to any form of feedback with fear. Any feedback is a potential source of physical or emotional pain, no matter what the source. Their first reaction is avoidance and self-preservation.

On the other hand, if they are initiators of feedback, they fear that anything negative they say will be as hurtful as what they experienced as children. They fear that they, like their parents, might lose control and become abusive. They fear that they too might become destructive to others. This results in a minimum of feedback within the group and the use of many passive-aggressive forms of communication.

All of this, of course, greatly hampers the process of communication within the group. If feedback is going to happen in a survivors' group, the leaders must focus their attention on it as a critical process and teach the group members how to do it. It is not going to happen naturally. Learning feedback skills must be a continuing process in the group. The need for them must be explained, and their importance and function within the life of the group and in relationships with others must be spelled out. We will discuss this further in the next chapter.

The dynamics of abuse have a continuing impact on the traditional intragroup roles of initiator, information giver, contributor, opinion giver, evaluator, and critic. Group members hesitate to accept any of the first four roles because a high level of visibility results, and being too visible in their families led to abuse. The first four roles make them vulnerable to criticism—in their framework, attack—from others in the group. They see the role of evaluator and critic as the roles their parents had in their families, and when that process began, it ended in abuse. They resist assuming those roles for themselves. They know how painful it can be on the receiving end of the process, and they also do not trust themselves to be able to control what they say.

WHEN DYSFUNCTION BECOMES DESTRUCTIVE

The complications we have discussed so far are interpersonal dysfunctions that can create communication and interaction problems within a group. However, survivors' dysfunctions can become more than harmful to group process—they can become destructive to the survivors themselves.

Survivors of abuse can become so mired in loneliness and low self-esteem, so overcome by their problems and the chaos of their lives, so confused by images and flashbacks of violence and misunderstandings arising from poor communication that they become deeply depressed and even self-destructive. Sometimes, as they explore their abuse, survivors find themselves becoming overwhelmed with negative feelings and filled with depression. The memories they have uncovered seem best left buried. The new feelings they have discovered are so frightening that they do not know how to manage them. They remember incidents that reveal the depth of dysfunction in their families and the extent of the violence and vindictiveness of their parents. They realize how distorted their experiences have been. The pain that has always been a part of their lives becomes more intense.

At this point, group members can become angry, depressed and even self-destructive. Group leaders may begin to wonder whether they are doing anything worthwhile and whether all the effort is really helpful. As difficult as it may seem, it is necessary to keep working on the abuse issues. Just as in individual therapy, things often get worse before they get better. Although it is important to be sensitive to and sympathize with the pain that group members may be feeling, and although it may be necessary to spend group time providing increased support and security, the only way out of the pain is through it. Leaders must help group members keep their anger focused on the perpetrators and the dysfunctional behaviors they seek to change, not on themselves. They must help them use their anger to challenge their pain and focus their energy on creating new options. To do otherwise is to allow self-pity and foster depression.

It is helpful to encourage members to express within the group their dissatisfaction with their process of growth and their uncertainties, fears, and anger. All of this pain must be articulated and taken seriously so that it does not become internalized and self-destructive. The group can be helpful in this process. Members can share with one another that they also have experienced such pain and frustration and how they have been able to break out of it. They can point out to one another approaches that have been helpful and those that are counterproductive. They can identify glimmers of hope that do exist, the little steps forward, the seemingly small signs of progress that only they can recognize as significant. The key to success in this difficult phase of treatment is to trust the process of exploration and confrontation through which each survivor must go and to help the group provide the reality-based support, encouragement, and guidance that only it can give.

The group can even be helpful for members who exhibit a chronic tendency toward suicide. Although the group leaders are responsible for assessing the seriousness of a suicide threat and need to take precautions to ensure that actively suicidal members do not harm themselves, the group can be a most effective tool for confronting suicidal feelings. The acknowledgment of such feelings within the group can legitimize their existence and break the taboo about discussing such ideas. Often, the sharing of such fantasies lessens their intensity. Such discussion can validate the existence of the feelings without legitimizing acting on them. In fact, group members can offer many reasons for not acting on the feelings. Their reasons may be the very ones that prompted them to resist committing suicide.

This can be an important time to encourage group members to reach out to one another for support. Group members may even be encouraged to contract with the group around self-destructive feelings and behaviors. A "no harm" or "promise to reach out" contract can build in a way to get support at the times a person is most in need. It comfortably authorizes the request for aid. The trust that is engendered when one is allowed to reach out and be supported and cared for goes a long way toward dispelling self-destructive tendencies.

Most group members are not going to be completely surprised when another member discusses suicide. Many of them have been there themselves. They can sincerely acknowledge the power of such feelings and understand the depth of pain from which they arise. They can also articulate reasons to continue to struggle, and they can address the futility of suicide as a solution by explaining that it is the ultimate surrender to control by one's perpetrator. Once again, group members can contribute more to dealing with these feelings than the coleaders because of the sensitivity and credibility they inherently have with one another.

❏ Summary

In conclusion, we have found that although adult survivors have many inherent difficulties functioning in a group setting, they also have a strong need and desire to be part of a caring, supportive community. Their longing for understanding and acceptance moves them to overcome their inbred isolation and their fear of rejection. But even after they begin participating in a group, many of their previously learned survival skills hinder their full sharing in the values of the group experience. Nevertheless, much of what the survivor needs to know and experience is best available through interactions in a group. The many evasive and manipulative tactics that former abuse victims developed (quite literally for survival) must be recognized as such, gently confronted, and carefully re-framed so that the skill can still be used when appropriate but set aside when not needed. In a setting where they can share with others who have had similar experiences, they can learn and practice the social and communication skills so necessary for happy and productive lives.

4

Strategies for Intervention

"In group, I started to change what I believed about myself and other people. And I learned I could express my feelings—even my anger—and nothing bad happened. In fact, I felt better."
—28-year-old accountant

"I used to think that making good decisions was a magical ability that others had and that I was just dumb. In the group, I found out that I could make good decisions—that it was a process I could learn and practice—no magic at all!"
—many, many group members over the years

There are many excellent books on group therapy that discuss structure, strategies, and procedures for such groups (e.g., McKay & Paleg, 1992; Yalom, 1985). We will not attempt to recap what has already been written in the field. We will simply focus on those aspects of group treatment that we consider especially pertinent to working with adult survivors of child abuse, that is, those factors that we believe make group treatment helpful for this population.

The chapter will be structured around four basic topics: structure of the groups, cognitive restructuring, affective healing, and behavioral adaptation. These are consistent with the intervention strategy that we proposed earlier in Chapter 1 and the goals for groups described in Chapter 2.

The Structure of the Groups section will deal with such issues as size, composition, format, and duration or scheduling of the groups as well as adding new members and facilitating termination. Group structure and operation are intended to address the needs defined in Goals 1, 2, and 3—breaking down isolation, providing safety and support, and establishing consistency to foster trust.

The Cognitive Restructuring section will focus on the distorted beliefs that are held by many survivors, and it will provide strategies and techniques for challenging these beliefs and promoting new ways of thinking. Under Affective Healing, we will consider strategies for enabling members to identify and express their emotions in a constructive and therapeutic manner, and this section specifically relates to achieving Goal 5—effectively expressing feelings. Finally, in the Behavioral Adaptation section, we will consider techniques to enable survivors to learn and test out new behaviors within the safety of the group. These techniques are especially relevant to Goals 4 and 6 and involve learning effective decision making and interpersonal skills. In these final three sections, we will combine discussion about technique with case study examples to clarify how the group process can be used effectively.

It should be pointed out that we see these groups as a conscious mixture of group therapy and support group. As Yalom (1985) has pointed out, all groups provide support for the members through the interactions between participants. Leaders should intentionally foster this interaction by promoting the sharing of experiences and facilitating effective feedback between group members. Such activities are essential for attaining Goals 1, 2, 3, 4, and 6 (see Chapter 2); achieving the validation, or legitimizing, of group members' childhood experiences; and overcoming the potential complications of group treatment (see Chapter 3). Cotherapists are necessary to manage and guide a volatile and often painful process that must be kept on track, but we believe that the support provided within the group by the group members is one of the most therapeutic aspects of this process. This belief governs our approach to structuring these groups.

⌐ Structuring the Group

A question-and-answer format will be used to address those questions we have been asked most frequently about conducting groups for adult survivors. Step-by-step recommendations with explanations and some case examples are included.

WHAT SIZE GROUP WORKS BEST?

We have found that a group size of six to eight people is ideal for such groups. Fewer than six heightens the pressure, and thus the anxiety, on each member, especially if anyone is absent for a meeting. More than eight increases the pressure (and thus the anxiety) on the group leaders. Because one member's revelations may trigger various stress reactions in other participants, having more than eight people makes it difficult for the leaders to keep track of what is happening for all members. A larger group also makes it more difficult for members to get adequate "air time" and to develop sufficient trust (always a difficult issue for survivors) for the group to do its work.

WHAT CRITERIA DO GROUP LEADERS USE TO DETERMINE WHOM THOSE SIX TO EIGHT PARTICIPANTS SHOULD BE?

The first criterion for this type of group is, of course, that the person is a survivor of some form of child abuse. Although some clinicians prefer to separate survivors of sexual abuse from those who experienced physical abuse, and males from females, we concur with Briere (1992), Gil (1988), and Sanford (1990) that the similarities in treatment needs are greater than the differences. We have also found that, although there can be transference problems when mixing men and women in groups, being able to work directly with this dynamic is fruitful for all concerned. Participants themselves make the final choice of what kind of group is right for them, but they should be advised in advance of the composition of the group. In the best of all possible worlds, there would be a variety of groups available for survivors—male, female, physical abuse, sexual abuse, and all the different combinations. However, the logistics of making too many distinctions eliminates the possibility of treatment for many survivors. We have also found that some people recall their sexual abuse only after they have dealt with the effects of being physically abused. We do not believe it would be helpful or good practice to tell them to change to a new group just when they are recalling new forms of trauma.

ARE ALL ABUSE SURVIVORS AUTOMATICALLY CANDIDATES FOR A GROUP?

In a word, *no.* All potential participants should be assessed by the group leaders prior to group membership. The usual contraindications for group treatment apply here: Clients who are "brain damaged, paranoid, hypochondriacal, addicted to drugs or alcohol, acutely psychotic, or sociopathic" (Yalom, 1985, p. 228) or those who manifest "active homicidal or suicidal behavior, active severe substance abuse, lack of motivation to change, dread of self-disclosure, a high degree of denial, paranoid, sociopathic, and strongly narcissistic or borderline personalities" (Courtois, 1988, p. 154) should not be considered for membership. In addition, people who are still subject to severe (not occasional or moderate) anxiety, dissociation, or depression when dealing with their abuse issues are not good candidates. Overly aggressive or manic candidates also should not be included.

WHO ARE CANDIDATES WITH THE MOST PROMISE FOR SUCCESS IN GROUP TREATMENT?

Group leaders need to determine that potential members have sufficient ego strength, ability to self-reflect, motivation, need, and interpersonal skills to benefit from a group (see Table 4.1 for screen-

Table 4.1 Suggested Questions for Screening Potential Group Members

- What are your reasons for wanting to join this group? What do you want to get out of the group?

- How did you hear about the group? Have you ever had a group experience of this sort or do you know of anyone who has? How was it?

- How do you feel about being here today?

- Tell us about yourself, your current life—family, school, work, friends. How are things going in your life at the present time?

- What was it like to grow up in your family? Are you in contact with your family at present? How do you feel about your family?

- How do you think it will be for you to disclose your incest experience in a group and to hear others discuss theirs?

- Have you ever discussed the abuse with anyone before? What happened? What were the reactions? How did you react?

- Tell us, in general, about your incest experience. Who abused you? How did the abuse begin and end? How old were you? What kinds of activities were involved? What were you told by the perpetrator? Was force used? How did you cope? Did you ever tell anyone or did anyone find out about the incest? Their reactions? Your reactions?

- How has it been to have us ask about these things and to be talking to us about them?

- How do you think the incest affected you at the time it occurred and since then? How do you think it affects you today?

- What are your feelings about being in a group with other incest survivors? What are your fears/concerns about dealing with the incest?

- Have you been in or are you currently in individual or group therapy? Tell us about that therapy—what is/was worked on, the therapy relationship, how you feel/felt about the therapy and the relationship, etc.

- Tell us about your medical history and any substance abuse problems. Are you currently in treatment for any medical/addiction problems and are you currently on any medications?

SOURCE: From *Healing the Incest Wound: Adult Survivors in Therapy*, by Christine A. Courtois. Copyright © 1988 by Christine A. Courtois. Reprinted by permission of W. W. Norton & Company, Inc.

ing questions). Clients' current life circumstances and functioning should be relatively stable. Excessive personal crises for members will turn the group into a crisis management process.

In addition, individuals need to be in a position to move forward in their lives beyond the effects of the abuse experience. They must accept the fact that the abuse occurred and stop trying to understand the reasons for this treatment.

> One of the few times we have had to ask a person to leave a group was a woman, Jean, whose only concern was trying to understand why her parents did what they did and why other family members, neighbors, and even the authorities did not make more of an effort to stop the abuse. Week after week, the group members offered a variety of possible explanations like, "Your parents did not know any better," "Your neighbors were afraid to get involved," "The authorities did not have enough evidence or enough legal power." Jean was never satisfied.
>
> The same questions kept coming back. We finally pointed out that without extensive interviews with the various people involved, it was impossible to answer her questions and that what was more important was that she deal with the results of the abuse. Although no one could do anything about the past and the lack of support given to her, the group could do something to improve the present state of her life.
>
> But whenever the topic shifted to her own present condition or to the concerns of other members of the group, Jean would simply tune out. After several attempts to deal with this behavior, it was decided, in consultation with her therapist, that Jean would no longer participate in group. Her therapist was to call us when she felt that Jean was able to participate effectively in a group process. That call has not come yet.

WHAT ABOUT THE USE OF INDIVIDUAL THERAPY IN CONJUNCTION WITH GROUP THERAPY? HOW DO YOU HANDLE CONSULTATION WITH THE INDIVIDUAL THERAPISTS OF GROUP MEMBERS?

The longer that we work with abuse survivors, the more we are convinced that the treatment plan of choice includes both individual and group therapy. Many of our group members are referred to the group by colleagues who see the benefits that only a group experience can provide. We especially encourage those survivors who are just beginning their recovery program to see an individual therapist in addition to the group. As indicated previously, the group often will bring up issues that require the focused, one-on-one attention of individual therapy. We always try to work in a complementary manner with these other therapists. We point out to group members the benefits of a collaborative effort between us and their individual therapists and obtain signed releases of information in advance so that we may freely discuss treatment strategies or concerns with their therapists. We insist that group members discuss their intended participation in the group with their therapist. Frequently, we are called by therapists who want more information about the format, structure, and goals of the groups. We welcome this contact and find that the open communication makes for better treatment outcomes for clients. In general, these contacts with therapists are on an as-needed basis. They are also another source of support for group leaders and a way to strengthen the resource network available to the clients.

ONCE THE SIX TO EIGHT MEMBERS ARE RECRUITED AND SCREENED, HOW IS THE GROUP STARTED?

We set aside at least 1½, but not more than 2, hours for the weekly sessions. We begin by asking the members to introduce themselves briefly, that is, simply state their first name and whatever information about their present family and employment circumstances they wish to share. We introduce ourselves in more detail, providing information about our professional experience, especially in the treatment of abuse survivors.

Then we provide each member with a printed version of the goals for the group from Chapter 2 (this also can be done on newsprint). These goals are discussed, and any questions about them are answered. We then ask group members to state the ground rules that they feel are necessary to ensure that the group is safe and helpful for them. These may be listed on newsprint as the members identify them. If the rules we view as necessary (see Chapter 2) are not forthcoming, we add them to the list.

This is a fairly low-key and intellectual beginning for a group, but we find that this helps members to relax and gently ease into a deeper level of sharing. At this point, we ask members to introduce themselves again. This time, they are asked to say as much about their abuse experience as they feel comfortable sharing, and to state why they have come to the group and what they hope to accomplish by their participation. The latter items are noted by the group leaders and recognized as the members' individual goals for group therapy. After this second round of introductions has been completed, we open the discussion to more general questions or comments, inviting group members to respond to what has been shared or note common themes and issues.

Generally, by this time members have achieved enough comfort with one another and feel such a sense of relief at finding people with similar life experiences that they are eager to respond to one another. The remaining time will be filled easily with this discussion. In the unlikely event that the members do not respond to one another, the leaders can direct the discussion by identifying similarities that they have noted between members' stories and asking them if they would like to comment further.

When there are about 10 minutes remaining in the session, the leaders should draw whatever discussion is occurring to a close and give each of the members an opportunity to make any closing comments they would like about this initial group meeting and to ask any final questions. The leaders should congratulate the group members for their courage in starting this process and thank them for the level of sharing that has occurred.

Group leaders also should advise members that they may develop some anxiety during the ensuing week about what they said during the group meeting. In the beginning stages of any group, personal sharing and disclosure elicit fear and anxiety. Our experience indicates that these feelings are especially strong for survivors. In the time between the first two meetings, many members have second thoughts about what they said, whether it was appropriate, and whether they expressed themselves correctly. Their fears about acceptance become magnified, and many times, the discussion in the second meeting is harder to start and maintain than the first. Therefore, group leaders should take time to discuss the possibility of this reaction and to assure the members that it is quite natural.

Anxieties about group treatment are common (Yalom, 1985), but such fear can be magnified by a survivor's abuse experience. A leader should encourage continued participation in a way that respects the intensity of the fears a survivor may be feeling. Members may find their anxieties paralyzing and believe that they are unique to themselves. The leaders will have to offer assurance that this is common and may have to offer step-by-step ways to overcome the fears (e.g., talking them through before the next meeting, talking with other members about their fears, meeting outside the meeting place so they can walk in together). If, on occasion, some individuals decide not to continue in the group, the leaders must reassure them that this is all right, that now may not be the right time for them to be in a group, and that the door is always open at another time. Emphasis should be placed on the attempt to participate in the group, not on the decision to terminate, so that individuals do not interpret their decision as another failure.

HOW CAN GROUP LEADERS INTERVENE TO HELP PREVENT GROUP MEMBERS' FEARS AND ANXIETY FROM INTERFERING WITH THEIR ATTENDANCE AND PROGRESS IN THE GROUP?

We encourage members to feel free to contact us especially between the early sessions of a group to discuss their fears. For those who seem particularly anxious, we may initiate the contact during the week. We also contact people who fail to return for the second meeting.

Sometimes even later in the life of the group, members' anxiety can rise to such high levels that they are afraid to come to the next meeting. (Causes of this anxiety are varied and were discussed in Chapters 2 and 3.) If a member calls one of the leaders to say that he or she "can't" come to the group any more, the leader can attempt to talk through the fears, provide reassurance, and encourage the individual to express the concerns at the next meeting and ask others for support. Because these fears are generally shared to a greater or lesser degree by all members, strong support and much positive reinforcement for returning to the group are offered.

If a member simply fails to appear, it is important that a leader call to determine the problem or concern. The member is encouraged to return to express the concern. This initiative on the part of the leader also lets absent group members know they have been missed.

HOW DO YOU HANDLE THE SITUATION WHEN A MEMBER DECIDES TO LEAVE THE GROUP PREMATURELY?

Sometimes, group members may feel that the group is not meeting their needs and may wish to terminate participation before their goals have been achieved. As always, we suggest that this concern be raised and discussed within the group. We ask the member to return to the group and state as clearly as possible just what those needs or expectations are. The hope, of course, is that alterations can be made to accommodate individual needs.

The individual's criticisms of the group process are often well taken. Frequently, other members will admit that the group was not fully meeting their needs or expectations, but they have been too afraid to speak up. Others may say that they have been aware of "something missing," but could not quite say what was "wrong" with the group. These discussions not only act as positive reinforcers for the group member who raises the issue but also serve to move group interaction to a deeper level. They also serve as living proof that it is safe and all right to ask for what they want and need, even if that means being critical. Finally, members can learn that positive, assertive behavior can be an effective means for getting what they want and need.

Another reason for having members discuss their intention to drop out of the group is to make it clear that their desire to leave is not the "fault" of any other member. Frequently, members will express guilt or fear at having said or done something in the group that they believe may have "hurt someone's feelings" or caused someone to feel "rejected." Even when a member misses a meeting because of illness, some group members may feel certain that the absent person has stayed away because of something they have said or done.

Again, it is necessary to reassure these people that their behavior was fine, that they did nothing wrong, and that they are still likable, worthwhile people. Thus, although this is difficult to enforce, it is worth the time and effort to encourage individuals to discuss their intentions and reasons if they are considering leaving the group.

WHAT IS THE FORMAT FOR THE SECOND AND SUCCEEDING GROUP MEETINGS?

We begin the second session by asking members to share any thoughts or reactions that they had about the first session during the week, such as any insights they have gained or questions that arose. This usually generates adequate content for the second meeting as group members identify insights and connections gained during the first session that excite or affirm them. If that question does not generate enough material, the leaders can ask members about the events of the previous week and whether they have issues or problems they wish to work on.

Subsequent group meetings are generally opened with the question, "So how has the week been?" or "What's been happening with you that you'd like to discuss with the group?" We quickly go around the whole group, giving everyone an opportunity to share before focusing on any one person's issue. Usually, it is possible to identify common themes (that is, the effects discussed in Chapter 1) that connect group members' issues, thereby involving more than one person directly in the discussion. Sometimes, of course, it is necessary to focus on an issue or concern that applies only to one person because it is an immediate crisis for that individual.

Regardless of the focus of the discussion, group leaders need to facilitate participation by as many group members as is possible. Questions such as "Has anyone else ever had a similar situation?" or "Do any of you have ideas you want to share about . . ." are helpful in drawing other group members into the discussion, and they also give members a chance to feel that they are helping one another. Such discussion also normalizes and validates the group members' experiences as they realize that they all struggle with similar issues. Often, a leader may notice a member nodding or being particularly attentive to what someone else is saying. Simply noting that apparent interest and asking if that person has anything to offer will frequently generate fruitful interchanges.

As this format suggests, we do not structure the content of each session, even though we believe it is essential to structure the process of the meeting (see Chapter 2, Goal 3). Although we point out common themes that are shared by members, we do not predetermine the focus of each session (unless it is decided that a topic will be carried over from one session to the next). There are, however, many group therapists who have developed treatment programs that have assigned topics for each session. Examples of these include Gil (1988) and Webb (1992). (See Table 4.2 for Webb's session topics.) Even if one does not use a thematic model, knowledge of the major issues or themes identified by these approaches can help leaders identify the common threads in the seemingly diverse problems of group members.

HOW DO YOU KEEP THE GROUP FROM BECOMING TOO FOCUSED ON "SURFACE" PROBLEMS INSTEAD OF DEALING WITH "CORE" ISSUES?

There can be problems related to starting sessions with a simple reporting of the past week's events. We have found that it is easy at times to fall into the pattern of discussing more current problems and putting on "bandages" instead of moving the discussion to a deeper level where long-standing issues can be explored. Although it is necessary to at least mention current problems of group members, if the discussion dwells on these, the group begins to function as crisis intervention.

A useful strategy is to look for patterns or repetitions in members' problems and trace these to specific behaviors that were developed as defenses or survival techniques during the period of abuse. This helps to direct group discussion toward core issues such as trust or the need for control. Focusing on deeper-level concerns also serves to include all members in the discussion because most can relate to the deeper issues if not to the specific event. Once members can define these issues and talk about them, they can move more effectively to change their behavior to avoid repetition of the same problems.

Another way to ensure that discussions of specific problems of group members do not become merely crisis management is to view

Table 4.2 Suggested Discussion Topics for Group Sessions

Building Self-Esteem	Learning to Trust Oneself and Others
Healing and Forgiveness	Dealing With Anger
Dealing With Feelings	Interpersonal Relationships
Identity and Entitlement	Sexual Identity and Intimacy
Pleasure (having fun)	Dealing With Conflict
Gaining Power and Control	Saying Goodbye (last session)
Problem Solving/Decision Making	

the process of any discussion as moving from the present incident to past causes and back to the present. The report of a present problem is treated as a jumping-off point for exploring past abusive experiences that may have contributed to the problematic nature of the present. The discussion then refocuses on the present incident, reframing approaches to the problem in light of the new understandings.

Focusing exclusively on the "problem of the week" can become oppressive. Sometimes, we have begun sessions by asking members to share one good thing that has happened to them during the week or to share one accomplishment from the past week of which they are proud. For many, this is extremely difficult, and they have to be prodded and assisted. Specific possibilities need to be suggested, for example, "What about that project you were working on?" or "What about the term paper you were writing?" or "Weren't you helping your neighbor with his garden? How did that go?" In addition to focusing on the positive, this strategy offers opportunities for group members to be supportive and offer praise and reinforcement to one another.

HOW LONG DO THE GROUPS CONTINUE? ARE THERE SET BREAKS OR A CERTAIN NUMBER OF WEEKS OR MONTHS?

We have found that most participants successfully achieve the goals that they set for themselves within a 1- to 1½-year period, especially if they are also involved in individual therapy. When we meet with them initially, we discuss this long-term commitment to themselves and the group. Sometimes, it is difficult for survivors to commit that far into the future, and often life events occur or responsibilities change and long-term participation is not possible.

We recommend that the group be structured for a predetermined duration (10 to 15 weeks) with a scheduled break. Seasonal breaks are generally the most common. They often can be scheduled around Christmas/New Year's holidays or the beginning and end of the summer when people often take vacations. Some groups and leaders opt for a 6-month schedule. This scheduling can be discussed with each group to match the schedules of members and leaders.

In addition to making the long-term commitment to the group more manageable, regularly scheduled break times also provide an opportunity to evaluate progress, introduce new members, and facilitate the termination of members who have completed their work.

HOW IS THE PERIODIC BREAK IN GROUP MEETING SCHEDULE USED TO HELP MEMBERS TO EVALUATE THEIR PROGRESS?

Group members should be reminded a week or two in advance of the final meeting before a break that this meeting will be a time to assess progress and determine new goals and next steps. At the meeting, each person is asked to offer his or her own personal evaluation. Group members are then asked to give each other feedback about the progress and growth they have observed. These sessions are particularly helpful because other group members usually see more growth than the individual reports. Members are then asked to discuss areas where they believe they still need work and to set some new goals.

HOW ARE NEW MEMBERS INTRODUCED TO THE GROUP?

Providing regular breaks in the group schedule also creates a natural opportunity for group leaders to introduce new members to fill the openings that occur as members finish their recovery work or leave the group for other reasons, such as job or schedule changes. As a rule, we do not bring new members into a group after a new quarter series has begun. Even if membership has decreased because of departures (unless it gets below five participants), we do not add new members until the next scheduled break. We believe that continuity and maintenance of the trust level are more important than maintaining the size of the group.

When adding new members, we follow a format similar to the first meeting. We ask the continuing members to introduce themselves to the new members first so that they model the kind of information to be shared. After the introductions, we ask the continuing members to discuss their previous goals for the group and the progress they have achieved. This helps the new members to get an idea of the kind of individual goals that can be successfully worked on within the group. (If there are only one or two new members, we do not discuss the goals for groups; these are discussed with the new member during the screening meeting.)

New members are encouraged to raise their questions and concerns about the group and how it works. Often, continuing members will recall their first meeting and the feelings that they experienced. Spontaneous empathy frequently is generated, and the new members begin to feel comfortable.

Adding members to the group can be anxiety-provoking for both the new people joining and those who are continuing. If the group process does not flow as described above, group leaders can facilitate some sharing by asking the continuing members to recall and share their own feelings, questions, or concerns from their first meeting. Or they can make general statements that normalize the anxiety, such as "It's kind of scary to start in any new situation, especially one where we're asked to share personal information," or "Even people who have been in the group for a while often feel nervous when new people join," or "I [the group leader] even get a little nervous before the meetings when we introduce new people because I want people to feel safe."

HOW DO YOU HANDLE THE SITUATION WHEN MEMBERS
COMPLETE THEIR WORK AND DECIDE TO LEAVE THE GROUP?

Obviously, group members do reach a point at which the decision
to end their participation is natural and healthy. They may have
gained sufficient insight and no longer need additional support
from the group. In general, we have found that most members
terminate after about 1 year.

Using the regularly scheduled break and the process of evaluation
provides the opportunity for group members to end group treatment as an intentional growth step. They can review the progress
they have made and receive praise and reinforcement from other
members. They also can be assisted in saying their "goodbyes," a
process that may be new and difficult for them. This process may
require some support from group leaders, who can help both the
members who are leaving and the ones who are continuing to talk
about their feelings. Generally, they experience a mixture of sadness,
loss, excitement, pride, and even fear—important feelings to process
within the group. Finally, the departing members can talk about
their hopes and plans for the future. This enables them to bring
healthy closure to the experience of participating in the group.

❏ **Cognitive Restructuring**

Because of their abusive experience, many survivors come into
group treatment with distorted ways of thinking about themselves,
other people, the world around them, and the interconnections
between all of these. They operate with distorted expectations and
dysfunctional perceptions. They manage their lives as if their abusive family patterns reflect the way the whole world is structured.
These thought patterns and beliefs must be examined, critiqued,
and, when appropriate, restructured. Examples of how this process
is accomplished will be discussed further.

A group setting is an excellent place in which to do this work.
Many of these distorted beliefs about themselves and others become
evident through group members' behaviors and interactions in the

group setting. The group provides a safe environment in which to challenge these cognitions and practice new approaches.

USING THE GROUP TO BUILD TRUST

One of the distorted beliefs common to survivors is that other people cannot be trusted; therefore, they must be continually defensive with all people in order to protect themselves. As we pointed out earlier, one skill that many abuse survivors acquire while growing up in their dysfunctional families is a highly tuned sensitivity to the moods and feelings of others. They often use this sensitivity to protect and distance themselves from others. The group setting can provide a safe place to challenge this belief about the trustworthiness of others and also learn to use this skill as a means for deepening their relationships with others.

For example, if a group member starts reacting emotionally, but nonverbally, to someone or to something that is happening or being discussed during the group session, one of the leaders can stop the group process at an appropriate moment and ask the individual to talk about his or her reaction and feelings. This is the first step toward uncovering the underlying belief that is driving the behavioral and feeling responses.

If it is too threatening to ask these questions directly, the leader might comment on what was observed about the person's behavior. For example, "Mary, I noticed that when Jim started raising his voice and talking about his anger at his father, you winced and physically withdrew into your chair. Right now, you look pretty frightened. Can you try to talk about what you're thinking and feeling?" What may come out are statements about people and incidents of the past that have shaped the group member's perspective and beliefs.

Mary might respond like this: "When Jim started raising his voice and I saw the anger and hatred on his face, it reminded me of my dad and how he used to scream at me. I felt afraid and I guess I started thinking that maybe Jim was like my dad, and in a minute he would start hitting me; maybe I can't really trust him either. But I *know* Jim isn't my dad and he wouldn't hurt me." Through this process, Mary realizes how she started to generalize her beliefs about her dad to Jim. She also is able to challenge this belief and begin to see that not everyone is like her dad, not everyone is unsafe, and not everyone is untrustworthy.

Reassuring remarks like, "It's safe to react and to talk about your feelings here in the group," can be helpful because they are the exact opposite of what was learned in the abusive family, where reacting or expressing feelings may have led to ridicule or physical violence. Statements such as this are a direct challenge to what these adults learned to believe.

Asking other group members to indicate if they share any of the individual's beliefs can serve as validation of the legitimacy of what was learned (i.e., most anyone growing up under these conditions would learn to believe these things). This also serves to open discussion about whether it is necessary, or makes sense, to continue to hold on to these old beliefs.

This process fosters the growth of trust between group members in several ways. First, the group member who is the focus begins to learn that it is safe to have emotional reactions and to discuss them with others. Second, the other group members experience vicariously the safety of the group, and their trust increases. Third, all group members begin to see more clearly what they have learned to believe about trusting others, and why and how they learned it in their families of origin; most important, they realize that they can challenge and change these old beliefs.

USING SELF-DISCLOSURE TO BUILD TRUST

Another way that group leaders can build the trust level within the group is through occasional self-disclosure of feelings or personal life events. Group members are amazed that people whom they respect and consider to be "normal" can have "negative" feelings and experiences. They are surprised to learn that disagreements and even anger happen in "normal" families and can be resolved without violence.

This kind of self-disclosure serves three purposes. First, the group members learn that conflict, anger, and other unpleasant experiences are a normal part of life. Second, they learn that such things can be resolved without violence or abuse. And third, they see that the group leaders are willing to share a bit of personal information about themselves. This sharing indicates that the leaders trust the group members. If leaders expect adult survivors to open up and share the deep, dark secrets that they have hidden for most of their lives, then leaders need to be willing to share a little about who they are as well. Effective use of personal self-disclosure can help educate group members, normalize certain experiences and reactions, and promote greater trust.

There are a couple of cautions about self-disclosure, however. Such disclosure should not be a weekly event; rather, leaders should be careful that their sharing affirms and validates the statements and experiences of the group members. Leaders also need to keep their statements brief to ensure that they are not drawn into changing the focus of the group away from the issues of the group members. Finally, leaders must also convey a clear message to group members that they are handling the situations that they are recounting. This lets the group members know that the leaders are responsible for taking care of themselves and do not need caretaking by the group, a role that is easily assumed by adult survivors.

USING THE GROUP TO BUILD SELF-ESTEEM

The group can also be used to challenge the negative beliefs that survivors hold about themselves because of the abuse experience. As group members come to know, like, and value each other, they begin to question whether it is valid to continue to believe in their own "badness." They begin to experience some cognitive dissonance as they find themselves admiring the strength and courage they see in these other survivors, and they realize that although the abuse was bad, it did not make those people bad. As they are able to separate the abuse experience from the abused person, they can also start to perceive themselves differently. As one group member stated, "If these other people in the group are really good people and I like them, and they were abused like me, maybe I'm not so bad."

These insights, or new beliefs, can be reinforced by statements of praise and support within the group. Although it is true that individual therapy also provides these positive statements, the effects on one's self-esteem are greatly magnified when five or six people are offering complimentary remarks and statements of respect and encouragement for one's efforts and achievements. They are also coming from people who are not professionals and who are not being paid to say nice things to the client.

REFRAMING BELIEFS ABOUT ANGER AND OTHER DIFFICULT FEELINGS

As discussed earlier, many survivors also hold distorted beliefs about anger and other difficult feelings. They have learned that feelings make people vulnerable to attack and pain, and that the expression of feelings, especially anger, results in violence and destruction or more pain and ridicule. Thus, they do not want to allow themselves to have feelings. It simply is not safe.

Frequently, leaders will notice that when angry or intense feelings are beginning to be expressed by someone in the group, group members will start to lose eye contact, squirm around in their chairs (and even move them backward out of the group circle), "shut down" or "check out" (i.e., dissociate). These nonverbal departures from the group process provide good starting points for exploring group members' beliefs about anger, hurt, sadness, and other difficult feelings. Leaders can point out what they see and ask group members to talk about what they are thinking. For example, "Don, I notice you started to stare out the window and drum your fingers on the armchair when Mary talked about how hurt she was feeling by her boyfriend's treatment of her. What were you thinking about? What did that trigger in you?" Don will probably respond to the questions with an old experience of his own, perhaps a time he was really hurt by someone. While listening to his story, members and leaders can try to discern the underlying beliefs he holds. For example, his apparent discomfort (as seen in his behavioral response) may stem from a belief that expressing one's pain is not safe, or makes one vulnerable, or is weak, or leads to embarrassment and more pain. His beliefs can be challenged as he sees how group members respond with support and caring to Mary, and how they also listen attentively and without judgment to what he is disclosing.

As group members learn to assist one another in constructively processing difficult feelings in the safety of the group, they learn that "negative" feelings do not necessarily lead to violent and hurtful behavior. Old beliefs can be challenged and changed, and they realize that people can be helped through bad times and that relationships can be deepened by such a process. This leads us into the next area of focus, Affective Healing.

❏ Affective Healing

One of the stated treatment goals for adult survivor groups is to enable and encourage members to express long-repressed emotions. This expression is part of the process of healing the "shutting down" or numbing of feelings, or affective dissociation, that so often occurs in victims of abuse. They have learned to deny, repress, or distance or detach from any emotional expression.

In the opening session of a group, this goal is emphasized. Members are told that no emotion is taboo within the group; all feelings will be respected, and group time will be allocated to allow for exploring the emotions associated with their abuse experiences.

Such a statement will not, however, immediately unleash pent-up emotions. As we noted in the preceding section, old beliefs are difficult to change. Because the families of group members discouraged and even punished the expression of any feelings, this is a difficult process to initiate. Too many messages to the contrary have been internalized over the years.

Survivors often are able to discuss the most distressing and painful events of their lives with no visible show of emotion. This obvious lack of any affect must be noted and pursued. Generally, instead of requesting the specific details of an incident beyond the information necessary to clarify what occurred, we ask, "How did you feel when this happened? How do you feel now while you're telling us about it?" The most common reply is a denial of any feeling related to the incident, or an "I don't remember." This statement may be totally true because of the strength of the survivors' denial or dissociative skills.

However, what we often notice as we ask questions about a feeling state is increasing agitation and anxiety in both the person being questioned and the other group members. Once again, nonverbal cues are very revealing. As we have discussed above, what these adults learned to believe at a very early age is that feelings are dangerous. They will allow feelings to surface and be expressed only to the degree that they can feel safe in the group.

One way to provide safety and help survivors begin to identify their feelings is for group leaders and members to "own up to," and acknowledge in the group, their own feelings about incidents they hear of or experience. A group member who denies having any affective response while recalling a traumatic experience is often very surprised to learn that others would feel angry, or hurt, or sad, or scared if they had been through that experience. The door is opened to beginning a discussion about feelings, not only for the person presenting but for all participants. As seen by this example, survivors often find it easier to identify feelings *for others* than for themselves, but that initial step can be used to help them get in touch with their own feelings.

Even if group members can identify feelings, they often do not know any appropriate ways to express them. Over and over again, feelings must be probed in the context of both present situations in the group and memories of specific incidents in members' homes. This will begin with intellectual discussions about which feelings might have been appropriate then and which ones still might be fitting, as well as discussions about how these feelings might be expressed.

Sometimes, however, all feelings are denied, despite the contradicting messages of body language and inappropriate behavior. In these cases, the leaders need to point out gently that certain feelings would surely be natural in this situation, and that such feelings are acceptable. This requires the leaders themselves to be clear about the possible range of emotions appropriate to specific negative or traumatic events. They also must be able to identify and discuss with group members the kinds of feelings that might be associated with such events. Furthermore, they should be able to describe the physiological reactions caused by various emotions. Finally, the important distinction between *feeling* emotions and *expressing* them needs to be emphasized. That is, leaders must affirm that *all* feelings are acceptable and human (even anger and rage); it is what we do with the feelings—specifically, how we express them—that may or may not be acceptable or appropriate.

Many abuse survivors have blocked their feelings so effectively that they do not even realize when they are experiencing a feeling. When this occurs, leaders might focus on the physiological responses and ask, "Do you feel tension in your shoulders? Or knots in your stomach? Do you get headaches? Do you find yourself clenching your fists until they hurt?" Once such physiological reactions have been acknowledged (and most group members feel more free admitting to such reactions than admitting to emotions that have value connotations), then their meaning and their possible relationship to specific emotions can be explored. This allows the group members to consider different possible emotions for a specific event (e.g., fear, hurt, anger) and become progressively more comfortable with identifying a specific feeling. As possible emotions are considered, the group leaders can be helpful by pointing out their legitimacy and noting that there is a wide range of acceptable and unacceptable methods for expressing each emotion.

DEALING WITH ANGER

Dealing with anger raises a distinct set of problems. In addition to believing that anger is inevitably tied to violence and destruction, abuse survivors experience enormous guilt if the anger they are feeling is directed toward their parents. They have been conditioned by society to believe that they are supposed to love their parents, not feel anger or hatred toward them. Furthermore, many survivors fear that if they were to start to express their anger, they would never be able to control it. They believe that the years of repressed anger may consume their lives, and that they will constantly feel angry at everything and everyone.

It has been our experience that this can be a critical point for many group members. Once an individual has acknowledged the anger and its legitimacy and has confronted the fear attached to the feeling, appropriate ways to express the anger need to be determined and acted upon immediately. The group leaders become key players in this process because they provide encouragement, support, and suggestions for appropriate forms of expression.

Sometimes, a thorough but calm discussion of past events and the feelings associated with them is enough. An initial approach to the effective expression of anger is to have members talk about ineffective, unsatisfying, or unacceptable ways in which they have attempted to deal with their anger in the past, including the denial of angry feelings and the refusal to express them. Such discussion usually results in the logical conclusion that anger must be expressed directly because it does not go away, and the price for keeping it in, such as depression or somatic complaints, is too high.

EXPRESSING ANGER VERBALLY

At other times, such a discussion will cease to be calm. Group members may break down in tears or break out in angry curses or both. The group leaders need to be understanding, supportive, and encouraging as they assure these survivors that such responses are necessary and good. The leaders may even suggest a few of their own favorite expletives for the occasion. Leaders can encourage group members to raise their voices or to scream if necessary in order to express their anger and release the tension it causes. Strenuous physical exercise, such as running, swimming, or biking, is also suggested as a strategy to relieve the tension between meetings.

EXPRESSING ANGER PHYSICALLY

Some adult survivors need to learn to express their pent-up anger physically. Usually, it will be up to the group leaders to suggest this possibility. It should not be forced upon the group, but it may be offered as an option. Specific suggestions can be made: throwing pillows and punching overstuffed chairs in the meeting, or setting up a punching bag at home.

Leaders should point out to the group members that at first they should practice expressing such emotions only in a controlled environment, such as the group. In this setting, people are present who can provide an assurance of control in the situation. They are available to help each other regain control should that be necessary. They can also ensure that no one gets hurt and nothing important is damaged or destroyed. In addition, in the group setting, people are present who can provide encouragement and support while the anger episode is going on and who can process and analyze the experience when it is over.

Group members may need to be reassured that this will not be a continuing and constant part of their lives. A few anger episodes will help them put the emotion into its proper perspective in their lives and enable them to move on with a new sense of relief and freedom. Although they may continue to experience anger about their past, and will most certainly find new opportunities to be angry in the future, other, more commonly accepted forms of expression, such as a long run or a vigorous game of squash, will serve to dissipate the energy and tension that accompanies the feelings.

Following is an example of how physical expression of anger was effectively and creatively used in one group.

Darlene had an especially difficult time dealing with anger. Anytime anger was discussed or expressed in the group, she became visibly nervous and tense, and she often pushed her chair back into a corner, cringing anxiously. Discussions in the group seemed to lessen her anxiety for a time, but whenever another incident occurred, she would become anxious again and huddle nervously in her chair.

Finally, the male group leader moved his chair in front of hers and asked if he could help her move out of her tense position. She nervously replied, "Yes." He helped her sit back in her chair and uncross her arms and asked her to breathe deeply. Then he held the palm of his hand open before her and said, "Darlene, please push against my hand." She looked at him with fear and said, "I can't do that. I'll hurt you." He reassured her, saying, "I'm only asking you to push against it. You won't hurt me." Slowly and tentatively, she began to push. With encouragement her effort became somewhat more forceful, but she soon stopped and said, "I can't do any more right now. It feels good, but I can't do any more today." The leader returned to his place and after a short discussion of the experience, the session ended.

In ensuing weeks, other occasions of Darlene's tense response to discussions of anger arose, and the same experiential opportunity was offered to her. Gradually, she began to push with some force, and the leader had to brace himself.

One day, the leader suggested that Darlene punch at his hand rather than just push. Her initial reaction was the same anxious refusal as before, but she did begin to punch gently. Over a period of weeks, the force of her punches increased to the point that the group leader finally resorted to holding a pillow from one of the chairs in his hand as Darlene punched at it.

After each of these occasions, Darlene had time to process the experience and discuss how it felt to exhibit her anger and then regain control. She also talked about who it was that she felt she was angry at—primarily her father.

At the end of one such session, she confided to the group, "I wish I had the courage to go over to the porno shops which are just a few blocks from campus. I understand you can buy life-sized inflatable dolls which are anatomically correct. I would like to buy one of those to pound on." One of the other women in the group quickly responded, "What kind do you want? Male or female? I'll make one for you."

The next week, the woman arrived carrying a life-sized stuffed dummy over her shoulder. She had received numerous startled glances from people on the street in her walk from the parking lot.

Max, as the dummy was affectionately named by the group, was the subject of much laughter and derision as he was passed around the group. It was also discovered that under the jeans that served as his legs, he was indeed generously anatomically correct.

After the group settled down, Max was set up in a chair and Darlene was encouraged to take a few jabs at him. As with the experience before, she started very gently and very tentatively. Gradually, the force and intensity increased, and soon she was screaming at the dummy as she struck and kicked it.

After a time, her anger was spent, and Darlene collapsed in the arms of one of the group leaders. "I didn't know how angry I was at him. I now remember many more of the things he used to do to me," she sobbed. After she regained her composure, Darlene looked around the room at the other group members and asked, "Are you all okay? I hope I didn't frighten you." They assured her that they were fine, and that everything was all right. She had expressed her anger, and no one was feeling any ill effects—except poor Max.

In the weeks that followed, Darlene had other occasions to attack Max, but they gradually diminished in frequency and intensity. Although she confessed to feeling almost constantly angry immediately after the first episode, this too diminished as she gained more control over her feelings of anger. She became more able to control and focus her anger.

This experience was very healing for Darlene, but it should be pointed out that simply venting anger is not enough and can even be dangerous. It is critical that the experience be processed in the group and that other methods for expressing anger also be identified.

Most important to note in this case study is that Darlene was finally able to get her anger out in a way that was not harmful to herself or others, and in a way that allowed her to be in control of herself even while expressing intense emotion. The release of this anger also enabled her to get in touch with other emotions she felt toward her father, such as her great sadness and feelings of rejection. Although these were painful to deal with, she was able to work through them with the group's support and care.

She also learned from this experience that others would not judge or reject her; in fact, they repeatedly told her how much they liked and respected her. Thus her expression of emotion was positive and reinforcing at many levels.

Group members who have gotten in touch with their anger and vented it in this way have reported a qualitative difference between this conscious, directed anger and previous instances when they had "lost their temper" and lashed out violently. Even though they direct their anger only at overstuffed chairs, pillows, or dummies, the new awareness of the true focus of their anger gives them more control in these settings than they have known before. Instead of striking out blindly, often at people or things that have no overt connection with the true focus of their anger, they understand more fully what or with whom they are angry and why they are striking the object.

They are conscious of the process of their anger—its rise, climax, and gradual diminution. They also have a sense of resolution. In previous experiences of anger, they often felt no real emotion and were not aware of what was happening inside them. They had never understood the connection between their angry striking out, their history of abuse, and their hostility toward their parents. They simply lashed out at whatever or whomever was closest at hand. As in the case of Karen (discussed in Chapter 1), who detachedly watched herself set a fire, they have no idea about the source of their violent actions.

The physical expression of anger also has a definite cathartic effect that releases a tremendous burden of suppressed energy. Abuse survivors report not only a relaxation of tension but also a new source of energy for other activities. They are surprised to find that after learning safe and appropriate physical means of venting their anger, they even feel less hostile toward their parents. They are able to deal with them in a more relaxed and understanding manner.

USING FANTASY TO PROCESS ANGER

Another way in which some group members are able to express their anger is to talk about the fantasies they have had related to their abusive parents. Often, these involve images of returning the physical beatings or emotional neglect that they have experienced. It may also involve sharing revenge fantasies. Supportive responses to this kind of expression are essential. Leaders must be accepting and understanding of these fantasies. Group members are usually supportive because they have had similar fantasies at some time in the past.

One man admitted that at one time he had been so angry at his mother that he had tried to poison her coffee. The mother smelled the poison and threw the coffee away, but the man continued to carry with him an extraordinary combination of intense anger and guilt from this incident. When he finally found the courage to admit this incident to the group, he was surprised to find that members were understanding and accepting of him. Many had fantasized committing similar acts. They perceived him as a victim who had been pushed so far and abused so badly that his murderous response was understandable.

Of course, the performance of such violent behaviors is not to be encouraged or condoned; murder or other physical harm to another person is not an acceptable expression of anger. Group leaders must always ascertain whether members are presently a threat to another and, if necessary, take appropriate preventive measures.

They must also help members understand the difference between having fantasies and acting upon them. But it is also essential to express compassion and empathy for the pain and frustration that could push a person beyond the limits of endurance and prompt him or her to contemplate or actually attempt such violent responses.

Finally, it is important to affirm the survivors' courage in sharing the fantasies with the group. Such feelings held in silence go untreated and are more apt to result in violent behaviors than are those exposed and discussed. As Judith Herman (1992) points out, "As the fantasies are shared, they lose much of their intensity, and the women are able to recognize how little they actually need revenge" (p. 230).

In the example cited above, the group responded in three important ways to this man's disclosure. First, empathy for his feelings and wishes was followed by statements indicating that he was still liked and respected—and that he was not an "awful person" for having attempted murder. Second, the members spent a great deal of time discussing the reasons that this violent response was not helpful or effective in "really getting the anger out," as well as the fact that the ensuing guilt over many years had been much too great a price to pay. Third, the group discussed other, more appropriate forms of response.

USING TEARS TO RELEASE ANGER

We also encourage group members to express anger and guilt, not just sadness, by crying. Many of these adults admit to not having cried since they were children. At that time, tears were greeted with derision or anger by parents and became associated with vulnerability and pain. They learned quickly not to cry so that they did not show their vulnerability or let their parents know that they had been hurt. Many have stated that as adults, they have "forgotten" how to release their feelings in this way. Furthermore, just as they fear expressing anger because they believe they will not be able to control it, they are afraid that once the tears start, they will never be able to regain control and stop them.

The following vignette illustrates the difficulty that group members have with this type of expression.

One young woman in particular felt a strong need and desire to cry, but she could not bring herself to the point where she could "let go." She had come to understand and accept intellectually that crying was all right and allowed. She trusted the other group members enough to allow them to see her in what she perceived to be a vulnerable state. She frequently talked about wanting to cry and expressed her frustration at feeling "blocked." The boundaries finally broke down during one group meeting when she began to talk of the intense loneliness and pain she had felt as a child, her response to rejection by her mother, and her belief that she was ugly, repulsive, and totally unlovable.

Her first tears were not a dramatic gushing forth, but rather a few painful, heartfelt sobs that were quickly brought in check. It was as if she were trying out the behavior to see how it felt and to see if she could regain control. Over several months, alone and in the group, she gradually became able to use the release of tears to relieve the tension and pain inside her.

Again, this experience taught this woman, and modeled for the other group members, that strong emotions can be experienced as well as controlled. Furthermore, the expression of these strong emotions can bring a wonderful sense of relief and freedom.

THE NEED FOR TWO GROUP LEADERS:
PROCESSING FEELINGS

Sometimes, group members will not admit to feelings they have within the group and will try to mask them. Therefore, it is important for the leaders to be constantly aware of how all the members might be feeling. This is another reason that it is important to have two group leaders. If a particular member or group of members is actively involved in a discussion or experiencing some crisis, one of the leaders can pay attention to that event while the other observes the rest of the group.

Even if members are not actively involved in the discussion, they still may be having strong reactions. The issue under discussion may be eliciting powerful emotions or triggering recollections and flashbacks from their past. The second leader can observe all the members of the group to note what else is happening and to focus the attention of the group on these other reactions when the time is appropriate. Two specific examples will help illustrate this point.

Carla had been an active and articulate member of the group for some months. Her comments and responses to others were always appropriate and helpful. However, the leaders began to notice a pattern. Whenever anything happened in the group that involved anger, Carla withdrew. If people were discussing their feelings about anger, she became quiet. If people were actually expressing their anger at someone in the group or their absent parents, she would physically push her chair back and grip the arms of the chair tightly.

With a second leader available to respond to these cues, we were able to question Carla about her behavior and gradually get her to discuss her reactions to anger. Initially, the discussions focused on her fear that any anger was ultimately going to be directed at her; therefore, her shrinking back was self-defense.

Gradually, it became clear that Carla was also afraid of her own anger. The anger expressed in the group often resonated with her own feelings. She wanted to voice her own feelings; she wanted to lash out with her long-repressed hostility. However, she was afraid of what she would do with that anger. She was afraid that even if she merely voiced it, she would lose control and begin to strike out. She was certain that she would never be able to stop. Her white-knuckled grasp on the chair was to keep herself from lashing out.

After much discussion and applying some of the physical expression methods discussed earlier, Carla soon learned to handle her feelings of anger and to contribute to group discussions about this topic.

Because of intense or fearful reactions triggered by group discussions about anger or the actual expression of anger in the group, it would have been difficult for one leader to have responded properly to Carla's anxiety. It might have gone completely unnoticed.

On another occasion, two female members of the group got into a very heated exchange. The discussion was fast and furious between the two of them. It took the full attention of one of the leaders to make sure they were hearing one another and responding appropriately.

During the exchange, one of the male members of the group, Henry, tried to contribute to this discussion. Henry is normally soft-spoken, and there was no way a quiet comment was going to be heard in the midst of this active exchange. Soon he became discouraged and withdrew from the whole process. He began to gaze out the window.

When the discussion finally concluded, the second group leader was able to ask Henry what he had been trying to say. He denied that he had tried to participate and said he had nothing to say. After some minutes of discussion, Henry finally admitted that he had tried to say something, but now he was too angry about being ignored to even want to participate. The people in the group were just like his family, he said. They ignored him and didn't think anything he had to say was important. If that was the way the group was going to treat him, he had "nothing more to say."

After extensive group discussion of the process of the previous discussion and of Henry's overly soft-spoken manner, and after some apologies from the two women, Henry was finally able to make his comments. He also came to see that what had happened was not a rejection of him, and that he needed to understand and accept group processes better and to assert himself more.

Henry's passive method of responding to his anger and frustration made it virtually impossible for a single leader to identify his need. He never would have had an opportunity to express his feelings unless the second leader had been available to identify his frustration.

USING THE GROUP TO SHARE POSITIVE FEELINGS

Appropriate expression is not just a problem with difficult and painful emotions. As we pointed out in Chapter 1, even positive emotions such as joy or satisfaction were often punished in abusive families. The exuberance of a joyful child was considered disruptive and annoying. Treated as a negative action, it was often punished severely. The message communicated was, "You should not be happy."

If children in an abusive family were successful at some activity and shared with their parents their satisfaction at a job well done, they were often ridiculed for thinking it was something important or punished for being proud and boastful. The message was, "What you do is not good enough, and it is wrong to feel good about yourself and your accomplishments." The ultimate message was, "Do not allow emotions into your life. They will only be the source of trouble and pain."

Given this childhood context, it is easy to understand why abuse survivors have trouble allowing themselves positive feelings as adults. They are reluctant to share their accomplishments with others and afraid to allow themselves to be happy. Therefore, it is important for the group leaders to program into the meetings some time when the members can share some of the good things that happen to them. As mentioned earlier, this can be done to open the session or as the focus of the discussion.

When members share their accomplishments, the leaders must respond honestly and enthusiastically. They must show true appreciation for what has been done and let the group member know that his or her success is recognized. Leaders should also elicit responses from other group members so that the person who is sharing can feel the full extent of that recognition. This process also enables all members to experience the feelings associated with giving praise. Such acts of positive reinforcement were not common in their families.

The group leaders also need to be alert to the tendency for survivors to negate their own accomplishments. Too often, even after someone's success has been acknowledged by group members, that person will be the first to denigrate it with a remark such as "It was easy" or "I was lucky." Leaders must challenge such remarks and reinforce the true value of the accomplishments. It should be made clear that there is no need to negate or deny what one has accomplished. Legitimate pride and joy of satisfaction are encouraged and will be supported. For one group member, this provided an especially moving experience.

> Kathy was a closet artist. She talked often about "my art," but few people had seen any of it. Frequently, members of the group asked to see her work, but Kathy would always "forget" to bring any. Even when the group leaders assured her that it would definitely be appropriate for her to bring her works to the group, she resisted doing so. Finally, one of the group members bribed Kathy by promising to perform a task that was difficult for him if she would bring in some of her work.
>
> The following week, Kathy arrived with a small packet among her books. She quickly put everything behind her chair. Early in the meeting, Kathy was asked about her art. Immediately she asked, "Do you really want to see this? Are you sure it's all right to do this during the meeting?" When she could not delay the inevitable any longer, she produced the work.
>
> The group members took a real interest in the work. Each one spent considerable time with several of the pieces. They asked how certain techniques were performed and how various unusual effects were

achieved. Kathy answered all the questions with a tone of amazement in her voice.

When everyone was finished and the works had been returned to their packet, Kathy was asked how she felt. After a long silence, she said, "I don't know what to say. You people actually looked at them. You took a long time with them. You seemed to be really interested. Nobody's ever done that before. This feels really good." The group sat quietly for some time while Kathy silently experienced the glow of an accomplishment acknowledged.

Sharing these warm, joyful feelings of appreciation and experiencing the gratitude of these courageous adults is one of the priceless rewards of working with groups of adult survivors.

PROCESSING FLASHBACKS

Flashbacks are a frequent and disconcerting experience for survivors of abuse. Courtois (1988) points out that participation in group therapy "usually stimulates the memory recovery as members 'chain' from each other's experience" (p. 299). This can be both a frightening and a reassuring experience for group members.

For some, it may be frightening because hearing others' accounts of abuse triggers similar memories that are new or more vivid than anything they had recalled previously. These new memories disorient members and often force them to redefine their abuse and themselves as survivors. It seems that the group is creating new problems for them rather than helping with resolution.

On the other hand, sharing flashback episodes can be validating and normalizing for those experiencing them. Members receive reassurance that such phenomena are not unusual or crazy; in fact, they are signs of progress in handling abuse effects. This occurs as members have more and more psychological resources to understand and manage the reality of their abuse. Members share with each other what they have learned from their flashbacks and how to contain them. They learn how to manage the timing of flashbacks and what happens to them when they do occur. They learn from one another the methods of control that are paramount to dealing successfully with abuse memories.

At times, members will experience flashbacks during a session. The other members of the group can frequently help the person manage the experience. However, the leaders must be sure that they have a sufficient "repertoire of containment messages and techniques" (Courtois, 1988, p. 299) to call upon if the group is at a loss. Various relaxation and focusing techniques can help a survivor feel safe, secure, grounded, and in control of his or her anxiety. For example, the person can be encouraged to focus on breathing, to maintain eye contact with group members, or to imagine a safe place. It is often helpful to remind the survivor that what is happening is in the mind and memory and that it is not the real experience. In fact, he or she has already survived the real thing, and this is only a memory of it. Often, touching the person (by the leader or a group member) will help the person connect to the present and feel safe. However, the individual's permission should be gained before such contact is made.

Sometimes, group members may wonder whether the new or more vivid memories that they are now experiencing are really their own or whether they are simply tuning in to other people's experiences. This raises a slightly different issue related to memories that are triggered in the group. When recollections are triggered by others' reports of abusive experiences, group leaders need to use care in processing this new material. Triggered memories do not always turn out to be about abusive incidents.

For example, during one group meeting, a member began telling of an abusive episode that started with her father coming into her bedroom. This triggered a similar memory from another woman (whose perpetrator was not her father) that was accompanied by feelings of fear. She immediately became uncomfortable and concerned that she would next "remember" her father abusing her. As we encouraged her to think back on this recollection, what came to mind was a frightening nightmare she had had as a child (the cause for the fear generated as she remembered the incident). In fact, when her memory of the incident was complete, she recalled how caring her father had been, how he had talked with her about the bad dream and consoled her, and how she had ended up feeling very safe.

Thus, group leaders need to be careful not to jump to conclusions about triggered memories. Recognizing the uniqueness of each person's history is important as members attempt to understand their own experience.

In any setting, memory retrieval is a difficult and confusing process. This is true even if the memories are positive and reinforcing. A person is trying to put together a jigsaw puzzle of his or her past with no picture on the box to provide guidance. In addition, the pieces are unclear and seem to fit together in different ways. It is important in this process to assure group members that what they are doing is an ongoing process. Pieces that seem to fit together one way on one day may fit together a different and better way another day when they have more information. They have to keep an open mind.

Furthermore, putting the puzzle together is not going to produce reality; it is going to produce a picture—a symbol of the reality. The importance of the picture constructed is its meaning to members as they reconstruct their past, reformulate their present, and create their future. Some of the memories may, in fact, be "symbolic manifestation(s) of a traumatic memory" (McCann & Pearlman, 1990, p. 31). The task for members is not so much to sort fact from fiction (something that is not always possible because external validation is often not available), but to sort reality from symbol and to ascertain the importance of the symbol, to determine how the meaning contained within the memories relates to their lives. Group discussions of the meaning-content of flashbacks can be especially helpful with this task.

Getting group members to discuss these memories is critical to helping them understand and gain perspective on the past and achieve resolution. The first step is to admit that the event actually occurred and to describe it or "walk through it." Next, the feeling-states related to the past event need to be identified. Owning the feelings and accepting them as "all right" is the third step toward gaining resolution.

At this point, the group leaders and members can provide therapeutic comfort and support. Finally, everyone in the group needs to reassure the person experiencing the flashback that he or she is safe and present in the "here and now." The past event is not really taking place; she or she has survived that experience. Over time, the flash-backs tend to decrease in frequency and generally lose some of their debilitating effects on the person, although they still remain as painful reminders.

It should be noted that this process will not provide information that will be acceptable as evidence in a court of law; that is not the intent. The concern in a treatment group is not to fulfill the rules of evidence but to help members manage and live effectively with the images of their childhoods that cloud their minds, confuse their feelings, and distort their behaviors.

❏ Behavioral Adaptation

Abuse survivors developed many skills in their families in order to survive. They learned to relate in certain ways with family members and others in order to protect themselves. They learned to operate according to certain roles and rules that may have been very functional in their dysfunctional families but are counterproductive outside that system. The group is a different interpersonal system within which they can learn and practice new behaviors.

LEARNING TO PLAY NEW ROLES IN LIFE

Many times, group members carry roles they learned in their families into the group and other aspects of their lives. They form alliances or define their role in the group based on their former family functions. In an abusive family, older siblings often take the greater share of the abuse in order to protect the younger members of the family. Many times, the parenting role is thrust upon them when the adults in the family are unable or unwilling to care for the children. They tend to continue this role of parent and protector, coming to the rescue of anyone in the group who is being pressured, thus interfering with that person's growth process.

These self-appointed surrogate parents also fail to deal with their own problems. Because the primary and instinctive focus of their concern is on the other people in the group, they are unable to pay attention to their own needs. Although these group members are often very mature and personable, and provide a great deal of assistance to the group leaders, they must be encouraged to deal with their own issues. It may be necessary to discuss their parenting or caretaking propensities with them so that they can learn to recognize these tendencies and consciously hold them in check while participating in a group where this role is not required of them. They must, in a sense, be taught to be concerned for their own growth and development.

Another family role with which many abused children are familiar is that of the scapegoat. This role may also carry over into the group. Unconsciously, most of the members expect at some time to be the scapegoat. They are internally ready for it, and they easily slip into behavior patterns that may elicit such treatment. Heads bowed, they accept any critical feedback as a negative attack that they deserve. Subconsciously, they may even wonder when the violence is going to begin.

To counteract this tendency, the group leaders must continually point out the scapegoat tone that group members project for themselves: specifically, their aptness for putting themselves down, their eagerness to apologize and accept blame, their failure to hear words of support and praise or deal constructively with feedback offered to them. The leaders must make sure that members hear positive statements about themselves. Sometimes, it is helpful to ask members to repeat back what they have heard someone say to them, especially when praise or support was given.

Confronting these stereotypes and rigid roles within the group is critical if members are to learn new ways of behaving. Members can, in fact, learn that they need not try to disappear into the background or control every situation by an incessant stream of words in order to be safe. They can experience being vulnerable without being belittled or being assertive without being attacked or ridiculed.

Specifically, we often ask people to try a new behavior for a meeting or series of meetings. For example, during one group meeting, we may ask that someone respond to the others only after they have correctly repeated the message that was said to them. Or we may ask a group member to be responsible for opening the next session and choosing the topic for the day. Whatever the specific behavior to be learned, we prepare group members by discussing the nature of the new behavior, the fears and difficulties that may be associated with performing it, and how these can be dealt with and minimized. Other group members often offer their struggles, successes, and failures with doing similar tasks. A plan is formulated, and encouragement is offered by all.

In addition to learning survival skills that are counterproductive in a nonabusive setting, many survivors also failed to learn many socially acceptable behaviors. Either they had no models for these behaviors or no opportunities to try them. As discussed in Chapter 2, effective communication is a critical social skill that may not have been learned. The first step in learning to communicate effectively is to admit the problem. We usually encourage group members to talk about particularly vivid memories of situations in which they felt afraid or socially incompetent. We ask for examples of ways they usually behaved in social settings. What generally happens is that members are surprised at the similarity of their experiences. They express disbelief at others' feelings of awkwardness because they frequently perceive each other as being adept at social interaction.

This recognition that others have the same uncomfortable and anxious feelings is an important insight. Especially useful is the group leaders' acknowledgment that they also get the jitters or feel nervous in certain social situations or when meeting new people. These discussions often conclude with members laughing at their own escapades and "social failures." This serves to release the tension and shame and helps them get to the point of discussing and attempting new ways of behaving.

We also ask group members to discuss events and situations that they expect to encounter in the near future, especially those in which they will need effective interpersonal skills, such as applying for a job, going to class, and attending parties or social events. It is helpful to have them fantasize what that situation will be like. We ask them to describe the setting and tell the group how they want to behave, how they expect to feel in the situation, and how they anticipate others will react to them. We also ask them to tell what they believe others will think or feel about them in the situation. This type of fantasizing about an expected experience in real life allows members to consider alternative forms of behavior before the event itself.

USING ROLE PLAY

Role playing is very useful at this point because it provides practice in what to say and how to act in initiating contact with others. To set up a role play, we have a group member imagine and talk about an upcoming event or situation. We ask this person to describe his or her feelings about the event and to suggest possible ways of behaving. Then, as a group, we hypothesize the potential response to these behaviors. Generally, it is not the desired response, so we spend some time considering alternate ways of behaving that may achieve the desired response. Several new behaviors are selected, and the group member is asked to act out those behaviors with the help of other group members. The "main character" determines all the roles and tells others how to behave, thus describing typical behaviors of others in his or her life. This process provides group members with additional information about the member who is the focus of attention. We also learn more about that individual's beliefs about others' perceptions. The following example illustrates the use of this strategy.

John, a group member, made a decision to confront his parents with their past abusive behavior. He had struggled for a long time with the question of why they had abused him. Although he did not expect them to affirm him, he had finally reached the point where he wanted at least to tell them that he remembered what they had done to him, and that he no longer wanted to keep it secret. He felt that in this way he could resolve the issue for himself to some useful degree.

The group brainstormed various approaches and tried to predict the results in each case. Then two group members took on the roles of the parents while John played himself and acted out what he would say and do. They tried several of the approaches and responses that the group had discussed. At the end of the role playing, he said he felt ready to go ahead and actually meet with his parents.

Several weeks later, he reported to the group that he had confronted his parents. The result was not particularly satisfactory because, as he had expected, the parents denied the past events. Still, he felt good about himself for having taken the action and even found some humor in an otherwise painful situation. He recalled almost laughing during the confrontation when his real mother's denial was word-for-word identical to that of the role-play mother in the group. The role-play mother laughingly pointed out that she had only repeated what her mother had said when she confronted her.

This example shows how the role-play strategy can help group members discover and practice new behaviors. This technique also provides them with the vicarious experience of possible responses and prepares them psychologically for the actual event. Group members may not always be as "on target" as they were in this case, and leaders may have to make sure that the full range of possibilities is explored. Even if the real-life experience is disappointing or unsuccessful, the role-play experience has prepared the individual for various responses and has made the other group members more aware of the individual's issues and feelings. In addition, having a warm, caring group that provides consolation and support helps to ease the pain and disappointment.

PRACTICING ASSERTIVE BEHAVIORS

Many abuse survivors need assistance in learning to behave assertively. Often, they will complain that "People walk all over me" or "I never get my needs met." When these comments are explored, frequently we find that these adults really have not asserted themselves when they have been passed over, or they have not asked for what they needed. The group can be an excellent place to practice assertive behaviors.

First, it may be necessary to distinguish between aggressive and assertive behaviors. Sometimes, group members are not sure where the line is drawn between the two because they are so used to witnessing aggressive or abusive behavior, so a discussion of the differences can be helpful in providing clarification. It may also be necessary to affirm that assertive behavior is not only appropriate but necessary in our society, where people are often too busy or too wrapped up in their own needs to pay much attention to someone else.

One assertive strategy that can be pointed out and practiced is use of eye contact when speaking to someone. This is often very difficult for abuse survivors, but it can be mastered in the group setting, where group members learn to trust and feel comfortable looking at one another.

Using body posture is another nonverbal way that group members can become more powerful and effective in their dealings with others. The difference between a body posture with slumped shoulders and downcast eyes, and a stance with shoulders held back and head up can be seen readily when demonstrated in the group, as well as the difference in the amount of personal power that is projected.

Practicing the use of "I" statements is also an effective way to increase assertive behavior. These statements can be made related to one's feelings (e.g., "I feel [angry, hurt, etc.] when you do [indicate behavior]") or needs (e.g., "Excuse me, but I was next in line"). Various scenarios requiring assertive action can be suggested, actual past or anticipated situations can be discussed, and assertive verbal and nonverbal responses can be practiced.

GIVING AND RECEIVING FEEDBACK

As we have pointed out before, giving and receiving feedback is a behavior that is difficult for survivors. Most forms of criticism in their families were emotionally painful, if not abusive or violent. They have not experienced feedback as a positive or constructive experience.

Therefore, group leaders must spend some time teaching and exemplifying feedback skills. They must clearly define the meaning and process of feedback, pointing out that it is possible to criticize specific behaviors of a person without attacking his or her personality. They must clarify the distinction between a person's behavior and how others respond to that behavior. Group members must be helped to identify their feelings about other people's behaviors and distinguish those reactions from the behaviors themselves. They need to learn to be specific in giving feedback and focus on behaviors or characteristics that can be changed. Both positive and critical comments need to be practiced, with the emphasis on what is seen and felt, not on judgments about motives. All of the standard feedback techniques ("When you say/do this, I feel . . .") must be taught and practiced.

Practice in receiving and responding to feedback must also be done. Group members need to learn to hear feedback as a description of what they have said or done and how it affected someone else, not as a judgment of them as people. And, of course, it must be emphasized that group members always have a choice about what they do with specific feedback. They may act to change a behavior, or they may decide that the feedback is not valid and choose not to make changes. Either way, there will be consequences of their choice.

One example where group leaders were able to compassionately model feedback techniques is illustrated below. In this case, a group member's behavior had become disruptive to the group process. The task was to continue to affirm the group member as a valuable human being while attempting to facilitate insight into his inappropriate and self-defeating behavior.

Although he looked about 16 years old, Tony was really in his mid-20s. He was working as a busboy at a restaurant while trying to finish his college studies. He was very quick to share, in a loud voice and often graphic detail, his experiences of physical and sexual abuse from a violent stepfather. But he met any attempts to discuss the emotional content of those experiences with bewilderment and quickly changed the topic to problems his friends, all several years younger, were having in their homes. Whenever discussion shifted from Tony and his friends, he promptly fell asleep.

In spite of gentle comments about the rudeness and inappropriateness of his behavior, this process continued for several weeks. The group leaders finally pointed out that the group was not geared to helping his friends who were not present and that discussion had to focus on Tony's needs or those of the people in the group. Discussion of the problems of Tony's friends was officially outlawed in the group.

Without the topic of his friends' problems to fall back on, Tony began to participate less and less—and to sleep more and more. Confrontations over his behavior became less gentle. These confrontations began to take up major portions of the group's time, and the hostility of the other members toward Tony grew.

The group leaders finally had a private conversation with Tony. Although he had little comprehension of why his behavior in the group was a problem, it was finally made a condition of his remaining in the group that between the weekly sessions he would meet with one of the group leaders to privately assess his participation and to identify specific behavior changes.

In these sessions, the leader talked with him about the level of his participation, his attention to other people's concerns, the appropriateness of his responses to their issues, and the specific ways he could change his behavior to participate more effectively in the group.

Although Tony never fully participated in the group during the several months that he was a member, he did cease to be a disruptive factor, and he did stay awake. Over time, he was able to pay attention to, and learn to hear and understand, the other group members' statements of need. They, in turn, received lots of practice in providing feedback.

LEARNING AND PRACTICING DECISION MAKING

One way that people gain control over their lives is through the decisions they make for themselves. For many group members, attempting to make even the most simple decisions about how to act or what to say are painful, difficult (and sometimes impossible) acts that reinforce their feelings of inadequacy and incompetence.

Group leaders can start the process of learning effective decision making by affirming that solving problems and making good choices are learned skills. This affirmation can be followed by a step-by-step model for making decisions or solving problems (see Table 4.3).

We find it most helpful to ask group members to talk about real decisions they need to make or problems they need to solve. Then, we start by helping them to clearly define the problem or the decision that needs to be handled. Next, we ask all the group members to participate in generating various alternative behaviors, strategies, or solutions. Sometimes, we find it helpful to have someone write these down or use a blackboard or newsprint.

The next step is to predict the probable outcomes or consequences for each potential strategy and to assess the advantages and disadvantages of each. Group members also need to determine the various skills, abilities, or other resources that may be needed for implementing each strategy and decide if those skills or resources are realistic or available.

After considering all these factors, a choice may be made from among the alternatives. At this point, they can begin to discuss how to carry out the decision and how to evaluate the outcome.

Table 4.3 Steps in Decision-Making/Problem-Solving Process

Step 1: Identify and clearly state:

the problem to be solved

the issue to be resolved

Step 2: Generate various solutions

Formulate different strategies for action

Step 3: Consider the potential outcomes/consequences of these solutions or strategies

Consider the advantages/disadvantages of each

Consider requirements of each (e.g., skills, abilities, knowledge needed)

Step 4: Make a choice of solution or course of action

Step 5: Carry out your choice and evaluate the outcomes

Step 6: (If needed) Reassess solution/strategy and make necessary modification

---

After a group member has acted on the decision, he or she can report back on the outcome. If all went well, the group will be a source of praise and reinforcement. If the decision was not able to be implemented as planned, a reassessment can be done, and modifications can be suggested. In this case, the group can be a source of consolation and encouragement.

What is most important about decision making and problem solving is that group members learn that there is a process for doing it that they can learn and practice. Over time, they are able to apply this process to other areas of their lives outside of the group.

PROVIDING SAFE TOUCH

Another behavioral issue that is often fraught with confusion and fear is that of touch. For many, being touched meant being hit; for others, touching was sexual abuse. And some survivors experienced very little physical human contact. Most people long for warm, caring, physical touch, but survivors are uncertain about how to achieve it and still preserve their safety. Frequently, this means doing without this very human need rather than risk a chance of being hurt or abused. This conflict was rather comically illustrated on one occasion.

> Barbara came to one meeting with a copy of a page from a magazine clutched in her hand. She played with it furtively throughout most of the meeting. Finally, she said, "I have something I would like to share with the group. I found this article in a magazine." She then proceeded to read a short article that maintained that people need six hugs per day to maintain good mental health.
>
> Sheepishly Barbara asked, "Could I ask if people here would give me a hug? I really feel a need for that. I'm way behind on my required quota!" The group response was overwhelming: "Of course, but only if we can all get one in return."
>
> From that day forward, every session ended with a "group hug." Everyone got their chance to hug every other member of the group.

This incident has been reported to other groups, and many have incorporated the "group hug" into their closing ritual. Group members have also reported that they have occasionally greeted one another in this manner on campus or on the street. The group leaders have sometimes been greeted with, "I'm having a hard day. Can I have a hug?" Such requests are never refused.

A group is a good place for survivors to experiment with various forms of physical contact. It is safer than any one-on-one situation because other people are present to ensure that it will not become inappropriate or unsafe. It provides an arena within which to discuss one's reactions to the experience as well.

Group leaders can help the members to establish rules around touch; for example, stressing the need to ask permission to touch someone, and reinforcing a member's right not to be touched.

Nevertheless, some caution and judgment need to be used relative to this example. This particular group had been meeting for several months, and members were fairly comfortable with one another. The issue of physical touching is a sensitive one for most survivors of abuse. Many cannot tolerate such contact. Their wishes on this matter should *always* be respected.

❏ Summary

In this chapter, we have described the structure and format of survivors' groups and provided some group strategies that may be used to challenge distorted beliefs and cognitions, reduce fears and promote greater ease in handling feelings, and foster more effective interpersonal skills. Our intent is that these examples be illustrative of the connection between beliefs, feelings, and actions, as well as of the value of a multidimensional approach to treatment of adult survivors. In the next chapter, we will look more closely at the role of the group leader.

5

The Group Leader

"At first I almost couldn't believe what I was hearing in the group. These people had experienced such horrendous abuse—and they survived to tell about it. I really have to admire them. I don't know whether I could have survived it myself."

—New group leader

"I have really come to appreciate the expression, "patience of a saint." If anything is going to make a "saint" out of me, it's going to be all the testing by group members to which my coleader and I have been subjected. Sometimes I want to scream. But I don't. I may achieve sainthood yet."

—Group leader

"One of the great pleasures (if it's okay to use that word here) of doing this survivor group has been working with my coleader. The challenges have forced us to clarify our therapy styles and become truly collaborative. It's been a gratifying learning experience."

—Group leader

skills and certain personality traits. All who have led such groups attest to the challenge and satisfaction they experience in this work. However, they also admit to the great amount of energy, attention, and patience demanded of them.

Effective leaders are called upon to be knowledgeable about the dynamics and issues surrounding child abuse, patient with dysfunctional relationship patterns, responsive to intense feelings, comfortable with their own feelings, and able to be appropriately firm counselors and facilitators of group process. They must also act as role models for adults who have had few positive adult figures in their lives to emulate.

❏ Knowledgeable About Abuse Dynamics

As one might expect, anyone working with a group of former abuse victims must have at least a basic understanding of the dynamics of family abuse. Leaders need not be experts on all the latest research on child abuse, but they should have a working understanding of the interaction processes prevalent in abusive families. They need to appreciate how these family dynamics tend to continue in later life and influence the former victims' adult relationships (see Briere, 1992; Courtois, 1988; Friedrich, 1990; Jehu, 1988; McCann & Pearlman, 1990). This understanding is particularly important if group leaders are to effectively handle the transference that occurs when members act out old family dynamics in the group.

This intellectual understanding and appreciation should not, however, be translated too quickly into an emotional understanding or proclaimed empathy. One of the easiest ways to earn the scorn and distrust of group members is to claim, "I know just how you feel. I know what it's like." This can bring sudden and sometimes vicious reactions like, "No, you don't and you never will. This has never happened to you and you can never know what it's like." Such responses are clearly justified. All the intellectual knowledge in the world cannot give a nonvictim a true understanding of the depth of pain and fear.

world cannot give a nonvictim a true understanding of the depth of pain and fear.

Abuse survivors do not want superficial sympathy or pity; they want an attentive and sympathetic hearing of their situation. They want to be heard and believed without horror or disgust and without judgment or condemnation. Once their situation is understood and appreciated, they can move to resolution of the feelings they have and solutions to their problems.

To facilitate this process, the group leaders must also understand the stages of growth and change that adult survivors experience as they work toward resolving the effects of their abuse. We have outlined a process of healing in Chapter 2 and referenced other models and ways to understand the recovery process. We believe that group leaders need a conceptual framework for their work so that they can be aware of each individual's progression (and regression) through this process of healing and can provide the needed support, affirmation, and encouragement.

❑ Patient

To be truly helpful, the group leaders must also develop a tremendous amount of patience as a product of the understanding and appreciation they have gained. The dysfunction engendered by a World of Abnormal Rearing (Helfer, 1978; see Chapter 3) is longstanding, and the destructive relationship patterns are deeply embedded. In turn, the process of change will be painful and will require time. Years of abuse cannot be healed in days, weeks, or even months.

Leaders must be prepared to accept and work with deeply ingrained behavior patterns that, although objectively self-destructive, were the ones the victims learned and the only ones that functioned well in their abnormal world. Victims do not easily recognize such patterns as "wrong" or inappropriate in the context of the world outside their abusive home, nor can they change them easily once they recognize the need to do so.

Many paralyzing fears and nonrational behaviors arise for former victims as a result of their abuse experience. Tasks and activities that people from nonabusive childhoods might find relatively simple and nonthreatening create major traumas for adult survivors. For example, the prospect of meeting new people can induce feelings of terror; the need to express their feelings, fears, or hopes, or the task of making a decision can immobilize them and render them literally unable to talk. Even the experience of success or praise can create major discomfort and anxiety for them. The leader must be able to appreciate the degree of difficulty involved in certain tasks and be able to offer sympathetic reinforcement and support.

TESTING AND TRANSFERENCE

The level of mistrust instilled in most adult survivors of child abuse also means that the leaders must be prepared to accept a tremendous amount of testing (See Chapter 3, the section on learning to believe that one is acceptable). Often, it will seem that the former victim wants to be rejected and wants the relationship to fail. This may, in fact, be a survivor's unconscious desire—it is a more familiar experience. Numerous trials will be imposed on the group leaders as the members try to determine the points on which the leaders cannot be trusted. It may seem as if members are unconsciously asking, "When will they become angry and maybe even abusive? What will make them dislike me and reject me? When will they recognize what a terrible person I am? How long will they put up with me before they give up and tell me how dumb, hopeless, and impossible to work with I really am?"

Sometimes, these questions are asked explicitly and repeatedly, as in, "Do you still like me?" Other times, the questions are silently implied and hidden in other statements, such as "Look at what a mess I have made of my life"; "No, I wasn't able to accomplish that (simple) task again." Whatever the form of the tests, the results are carefully tabulated. No matter what the method of inquiry, the leader must be prepared to answer patiently with constant reinforcement and reassurance. The reassurance must be genuine and strong because it must penetrate the screen of a predetermined sense of rejection and disbelief.

Inherent in this testing is the process of transference. As one might expect, survivors of abuse have a great deal of residual fear, dislike, and anger toward their abusive parent. These feelings frequently get directed toward whichever group leader most nearly resembles that parent. Therefore, the forms of testing administered to leaders vary greatly depending on the gender of the leader. Also, the degree of a leader's acceptance or rejection by a group member varies according to the same factor. This is a major reason why we insist on one male and one female leader for each group. There must be opportunity for the different transferences to be resolved. Group leaders must be prepared to accept and work with these transference dynamics.

It is easy to understand, and even expect, that the leader who is the same gender as the abusive parent will receive some negative transference and testing. This testing, however, will not be limited to that leader. As much, if not more, testing and hostility may be directed at the leader representing the nonabusive parent. Victims feel a great deal of anger and distrust toward the parent who did not protect them. Generally, this anger is not as conscious or clearly defined as the anger toward the abusive parent. Therefore, the leaders will have to allot a great amount of time, patience, and careful analysis to helping the group members understand and acknowledge this aspect of their anger.

This problem may become even more complicated if the non-abusive parent was also victimized. In such a case, that parent may be idealized. Even though he or she did not protect the child, the parent is seen as a fellow victim and even a martyr. That ideal image is then transferred to the same-gender leader, with the result that this leader can do or say nothing wrong, and the other can say nothing right.

The following case study indicates one way we have worked with this transference process.

Roger was the victim of an especially violent father. Beatings were frequent and brutal, occasionally resulting in the need for medical treatment. Although Roger was most often the victim of the attacks, his mother was also beaten. She apparently took the beatings passively and without complaining.

When Roger talked about his father, he himself became violent, stamping his feet, pounding the arms of his chair and cursing loudly. However, any mention of his mother immediately calmed him. He talked softly and gently about what a dear, sweet woman she was and how she had been "a living saint to put up with that bastard." Any attempt to discuss why she had stayed in the relationship and allowed the beatings of both of them to go on was dismissed: "She couldn't help it. He was too big."

From his very first meeting, Roger was drawn to the female leader of the group. He was attentive to anything she said or did, complimenting her on her appearance as well as on any comments she made. Whenever possible, he would sit next to her. None of the other women received similar attention. At the end of each meeting, Roger would thank the leader profusely for her help and support. Usually, these comments were accompanied by remarks about how much she reminded him of his mother.

On the other hand, his reaction to the male leader was exactly the opposite. He would sit as far away from him as possible and turn his chair away. He dismissed the male leader's comments, and no matter what had transpired during the meeting, Roger usually concluded the session by saying he did not think the male leader liked him.

After this had gone on for several weeks, with Roger making very little progress in dealing with his own problems, the leaders decided to try the "good guy, bad guy" team approach. The female leader took on the "bad guy" role with the responsibility of offering critical feedback and pressuring Roger for more change and response. The male leader, already cast in the "bad guy" role, was to take on the task of being the sensitive, sympathetic, and supportive "good guy." No matter what the need for criticism or pressure, the male leader was to leave all of that to the female and simply compliment and praise Roger for whatever he had done well.

This plan was carried out for some weeks but Roger's responses did not change. The female leader would provide very specific feedback about the negative effects of Roger's behavior. She would push him to take responsibility for his actions and their effects. She even confronted him with the incongruency of what she was telling him and how he was responding, all to no avail. It was as if he wasn't hearing her words, only reacting to her as a woman. At the end of each session, he thanked her and praised her profusely. And he continued to attack the male leader for his lack of sensitivity.

In time, other group members were noting and pointing out Roger's misperceptions. People were coming to the defense of the male group leader. Roger was finally forced to make some distinctions between his father and other men in authority and between his mother and other women in authority.

At last, he toned down his respective praise and criticism, his more explicit forms of transference. However, in the remaining weeks until the group disbanded for the summer, Roger never really changed his nonverbal responses to the two leaders. It was as if he could not break free from his rigid beliefs about men and women and their behavior toward him.

This orchestration procedure, although only mildly successful, was one attempt to use the transference process as a means of therapy for a group member. Transference is certain to occur; the leaders must be prepared for and must patiently work through this long and complicated process.

EVASION AND MANIPULATION

Other interpersonal strategies learned in an abusive family that require understanding and great patience on the part of the leaders are evasion and manipulation. These strategies usually have negative connotations in our culture. Manipulative and evasive people are thought to be up to no good, trying to get something they do not deserve, or to get out of something they do deserve. For those who grew up in an abusive home, however, these are basic and essential survival skills. These are the methods they learned to avoid the abuse they did not deserve, and to get the attention and caring that should have been theirs automatically.

The problem is that these skills are now almost instinctive for former victims. They use them without thinking. They apply them to situations in which they are no longer necessary or appropriate. As we discussed in Chapter 3, these methods may even be counterproductive to what the former victim really wants to accomplish. Use of manipulative and evasive strategies in communicating often results in distortion of the very important messages that the individual wants to convey.

In the efforts to change these deeply ingrained behavior patterns, leaders must be ready to provide careful and patient analysis of present behavior, to point out the ineffectiveness of that behavior in most present situations, and to help members develop and practice new forms of behavior. Because deeply ingrained and previously vital instincts are being challenged, they will not be quickly or easily reformed.

❏ Responsive to Feelings

Adult survivors of abuse quite naturally have many emotions related to their abusive experience. Unfortunately, they generally are not in touch with their feelings. The emotions are deep and pervade all aspects of their life, but they are ill-defined and often associated with extreme guilt. These emotions are strong and often are inappropriately directed or expressed.

As we pointed out in Chapter 2 on group goals, one of the major tasks of group therapy is to help the members get in touch with their own feelings. The leaders must make this clear at the outset by emphasizing that it is expected that group members will experience strong feelings and that expression of these emotions will be supported and encouraged. No emotion is considered taboo, and all emotions will be respected. The role of the leaders is to help the group discuss and process these emotions and find appropriate and effective ways to express them.

❏ Comfortable With Our Own Feelings

To be supportive of this kind of process, it is clear that the group leaders must be comfortable with their own emotions and with allowing others to express theirs. They must validate their verbal statements about the acceptability of all emotions through their attitudes and actions within the group. Thus, emotional expression must be allowed to run its full course and not be cut off prematurely. Probing questions that enable group members to safely explore emotion-laden issues need to be asked with sensitivity and confidence. Leaders need to be clear about how they are affected by expression of intense emotions, especially anger and deep pain.

They need to recognize the limits of their own tolerance and be able to set clear boundaries.

This clarity is also important if leaders are to be sensitive enough to support those in the group who may be frightened by expressions of anger. Many group members will react to someone else's anger with fear. They may be immediately convinced that they are at fault and that they are the object of the anger. They may even expect to be physically attacked, because this has been their previous experience. So they need frequent reassurance and comfort. The leaders must be able to ensure safety for all while supporting the expression of anger by a group member. The leaders must point out the real reasons for the anger and must emphasize that the members are not a part of those reasons.

BEING HONEST ABOUT OUR FEELINGS

The group leaders also must be honest about their own emotions. There will be times in the group when the slow pace of members' development, the manipulative and evasive tactics, and the frequent testing will put a severe strain on the leaders' frustration tolerance. These are normal countertransference feelings.

Because former victims possess a high level of sensitivity, they will quickly note any frustration, exasperation, or anger. Most often, the group members will not raise the issue and confront it but will simply internalize the leaders' frustration as another message about how "bad" they (the members) are. Therefore, the group leaders must be aware of their own feelings and be quick to acknowledge them to the group; then the feelings and their causes can be discussed. The leaders can use this opportunity to illustrate how they may be frustrated by a person's behavior but still continue to like and accept the person, and the group can deal with the sources of the anger or frustration.

Every experienced group leader realizes that not all the frustration that he or she may feel during a group meeting originates in the group. Pressures and tensions of everyday life overflow into the group even for the most experienced group leader. These feelings are also perceived by the group members, but they may well believe that they are the cause of them. Therefore, it is also necessary to acknowledge such concerns to the group, "My kids have been a pain this week," "My job is driving me crazy," "My husband and I had an argument last night." As we discussed earlier in Chapter 3, this not only serves to clear the air and confirm for group members that they are not at fault, it also provides some important role models for them to follow. Such sharing by leaders has often been the starting point for fruitful discussions, such as those described in Chapter 4. However, no such discussions will take place unless the group leaders are aware of their feelings and are willing to share them with the group.

DEALING WITH THE PAIN AND SORROW OF GROUP MEMBERS

Group leaders also must be prepared to support members in their pain. Sorrow is an emotion that adult survivors frequently need to express. They have repressed, denied, or minimized much disappointment and anguish over the years. Providing effective support may involve touching and physical contact.

Many former victims have a great need for someone who can comfort them in their sorrow and grieving. Until now, most of their tears have been solitary ones. Although they cannot consciously ask for it, many of them hunger for some form of soothing contact, a hand to clasp, an arm around the shoulder, a warm embrace. Leaders must be able to read the nonverbal cues to know when to initiate such contact, taking care always to ask permission before actually touching someone. They must also be able to read past the verbal messages that say "Don't touch me" to the probable ambivalence related to physical warmth and contact. For many formerly abused children, physical contact was a painful experience. They cannot believe that it can be soothing and comforting, even though they desperately want it to be so.

Once again, the group leaders must be comfortable enough with themselves and clear about their personal boundaries so that they may respond to the needs of group members for physical warmth and offer a reassuring hand clasp or a comforting embrace. Actually, the group is the safest and most helpful place for such contact to take place. Members' fears of possible sexual overtones and connotations are minimized by the presence of other people, and the embarrassment about feeling such a need can be assuaged by the reassurances of other group members.

❏ The Issue of Abuse

Another area where the group leaders must also know themselves and be aware of their own feelings concerns the issue of abuse itself. They must be able to react with sensitivity to the accounts of abuse that they are going to hear, but they should not overreact. Expressions of horror or disbelief are not helpful to the former victims. They already know how horrible it was. They do not have to be reminded, and they do not want their accounts to be a source of distress for the very people who are trying to help them.

On the other hand, the leaders must make it clear to the group members that they understand the nature of the abuse that occurred and that they accept and appreciate the anger and hostility the former victims may be expressing. This is necessary if any level of trust is going to be established. Many group members who have sought private counseling regarding their abuse have had negative experiences. Counselors have rejected or ridiculed their accounts, or they have dismissed the connection between the past abuse and present problems. Too often, the former victim has been told, "That happened 15 years ago; it has nothing to do with your problem now. Forget about it." Such a response on the part of a helping professional makes the next therapist's job of earning trust an uphill battle.

BEING AWARE OF OUR COUNTERTRANSFERENCE

Most leaders will experience a lot of anger toward the parents of the people with whom they are working. Such anger, another form of countertransference, is appropriate and should be expressed, but in such a way that it does not demand a similar reaction from the former abused child. The leaders must own their own feelings and not impose them on the survivor. He or she may not be ready yet to deal with that long-repressed anger. Seeing that someone else is angry about what happened can be a freeing experience, but it also may be frightening. Instant liberation or agreement should not be expected. Also, the leaders need to be careful not to overdo the intensity of the feeling because this may cause the survivor to believe that he or she isn't even able to "feel his or her feelings correctly."

Furthermore, many survivors of abuse need and want to maintain a relationship with their parents. No matter what their parents did to them, they are still their parents, and that bond needs to be preserved. Overly negative and judgmental remarks about their parents can make members feel they should hate them and sever all relationships. Even if this were physically possible, it might well destroy their last sense of contact with a family, no matter how poor that might have been.

To be effective, group leaders must maintain a neutral stance toward parents, even if they feel anger or hostility because of what they have heard. As discussed earlier, the distinction needs to be made between a person's actions or behavior and the person as an individual. Leaders need to assist group members in assessing their relationships with their parents. This involves considering what, if anything, their parents did that was helpful and what was abusive, both in the past and in the present-day relationship. Members need help in determining what they want to confront about the past (or present) and what they will choose to let go of. Most important for many group members is reaching a decision about what level of contact or type of relationship is necessary, desirable, or even possible with their parents. Group leaders need to be supportive of group members and nonjudgmental of group members' parents if they are to be effective in these analysis, clarification, and decision-making processes. Finally, they need to be able to assist in developing healthy behavioral strategies to continue or end contact or relationships with parents.

Frequently, members need to maintain this contact at a distance by making separate living arrangements, visiting only infrequently and under carefully controlled circumstances, and preparing themselves emotionally beforehand. Although such visits may seem contrived or forced to an outsider, it may well be the only type of family contact the abuse victim can deal with comfortably. Thus, it needs to be maintained.

On at least one occasion, a member's need to maintain a semblance of family life caused an unusual form of stress for one group leader:

> Denise participated in a group for a full school year. Her accounts of extreme physical and sexual abuse involving both of her parents were shared only with great difficulty. However, with the help of the group as well as a private therapist, she was able to resolve many of her personal and sexual identity questions. When the group reconvened for the next school year, she decided that she did not need to participate.
>
> Late in that second year, there was a special dinner on campus to which parents were invited. Halfway through the evening, Denise approached one of the leaders, who was attending the dinner. She had brought her parents, and she wanted him to meet them. She introduced him as the campus minister with whom she had worked on many projects. Her parents were very well dressed, both in tailored suits. They and the leader had a pleasant conversation for several minutes about their respective professions and their involvement in local church projects. They exchanged long lists of names of clergy with whom they had all worked at one time or another. The conversation ended cordially with warm handshakes all around.
>
> This incident lasted only 15 minutes, but the cognitive dissonance made it seem like hours. This leader was meeting and conversing with a set of parents who were evidently successful professionals, active church members, and respected participants in their community; yet he was aware that they had also performed some of the worst forms of child abuse he had ever heard. The internal discord was tremendous.

The leader gained a new appreciation of why Denise had difficulty getting assistance from her pastor and her school counselors when she had approached them as a teenager. Her parents fit none of the stereotypes associated with child abuse. Her accusations had been dismissed as the ranting of a confused adolescent. The leader might have been similarly inclined had he not been aware of the anguish and pain involved in Denise's earlier disclosures. Despite the discomfort the leader experienced, it was important to Denise that her parents be treated with courtesy and respect.

❏ Survivors as Group Leaders

The question has sometimes been raised whether former abuse victims themselves can be group leaders or whether all leaders should be abuse survivors. This is a complex issue. One woman who contacted us about joining a group changed her mind because the leaders were not survivors of abuse. She did not believe that someone who had not been victimized could adequately understand or treat someone who had been abused. In fact, at times, abuse survivors have served as leaders of groups in our program, but this experience has had both positive and negative aspects.

Despite the one woman's insistence that a nonsurvivor could not help her, those leaders who are survivors have reported that at least initially, some of the group members tended to look more to the other, nonsurvivor leader for guidance and support. This perception was confirmed by the nonsurvivor leader. It seemed as if another abuse survivor, even though a leader of the group, could not provide the same insight and guidance as someone who had "normal" childhood experiences. The initial assumption seemed to be, "If you had the same experiences as I did, you must be as "bad" as I am and have the same problems I do. Therefore, I can't value your advice as highly as that of the other leader." However, those reporting also pointed out that this distinction between leaders diminished quickly and that group members soon came to respect and value the guidance and support of both equally. The leader who was a survivor became a strong role model for what it is possible to attain. Nevertheless, the initial response had to be taken into consideration.

On the other hand, there is a certain validity to the woman's desire to have an abuse survivor as a group leader. Those who have not suffered abuse cannot fully understand or appreciate the experiences that survivors have had and the difficulties they continue to face. Someone who has not been victimized can learn to understand intellectually what an abuse survivor has experienced, but can never fully appreciate the terror and anguish, the shame and guilt, and the profound sense of self-deprecation that abuse can engender.

Again and again, group members have responded angrily to our prodding and pressure for change: "You don't know how it feels!";

"You don't know how difficult this is to do!" Our answer has simply been, "You're right. I don't know. I know how I feel when you tell me about it, but I have never experienced it myself. I can't really know what it's like. I am sorry about the pain this may be causing you. But that doesn't deny the need for you to make this change (try this behavior, talk about this problem)."

In short, we have no simple answer to the question of survivor versus nonsurvivor leaders. There are pros and cons on both sides. However, our experience on a very practical level says that it is difficult to find enough group leaders of either kind to meet the demand. The question that must be asked of group leaders who do not have a history of abuse is whether they can be understanding and empathic enough to gain the confidence of the group members.

For leaders who are survivors of abuse, the questions include whether they have resolved their own issues resulting from their abuse and whether they have clarified their feelings about themselves and their parents. Are they able to achieve adequate distance from their own experience so that they do not confuse their own emotions and experiences with those of the members of the group? Have they reclaimed the power that was lost because of the abuse experience and taken control of their lives? If they have accomplished these tasks, then they clearly have the edge over a nonvictim leader in understanding and appreciating the ramifications of an abusive past. Still, we must remember that every person's experience is unique, and one's history (whether abusive or nonabusive) does not guarantee, nor does it limit, one's ability to be empathic and supportive of group members' efforts at growth and change.

❏ Providing Structure and Firm Guidelines

Thus far, we have described group leaders as people who must be knowledgeable, empathic, and supportive. These qualities are essential, but this does not mean leaders can be soft-touch pushovers. While being sympathetic and sensitive, they must also be clear about their objectives for the group and its members and firm enough to carry out those goals.

One of the first issues about which they must be clear is the structure and direction of the group. As we have noted, those who grow up in dysfunctional, violent families are accustomed to functioning in chaos and may, therefore, be more comfortable in such an environment. This means it may take a special effort on the part of the leaders to develop and maintain a structure for the group.

It is particularly important to begin with a tight structure, which can be relaxed later. It is very difficult to impose a firm structure after a group has been functioning without one. The advantages, as well as the complications, of providing firm structure have already been discussed in Chapter 4.

Another area where gentle firmness is especially necessary is in the process of supporting group members as they struggle to change destructive behaviors and to grow. This requires an especially delicate sensitivity to the deeply ingrained fears that the members of the group have developed because of their abusive experiences. Most of their previous experiences of criticism and correction have taken the form of nagging at best and physical abuse at worst. Any criticism is seen as a prelude to violence. Any critic is viewed as a potential abuser. Therefore, anything that bears a resemblance to previous experience is immediately tuned out, and the source of the critique is categorized with their parents. A great deal of patient interpretation and gentle repetition is necessary to get beyond this blockage. Clear and forthright statements distinguishing what is said and done now from what was said and done in the past must be made repeatedly.

It is important in this process to be constantly reassuring about one's affection for the group member even as one presses for change. The role of the leader is to help the group member to identify the patterns of behavior that are causing problems (or unwanted consequences) and to assist the individual in understanding what function the behavior serves (either now or in the past) and why it developed. Often, as these insights are gained, group members actively seek assistance in learning new ways of behaving. The leader must emphasize that even if the desired result is not achieved, the relationship and the affection for the group member will remain the same. During this process, the leaders must be consistent in the desires and expectations they express, as well as the affection they offer; this is essential to maintaining a trusting relationship.

Another distinction that leaders must constantly clarify and reinforce is the difference between accepting someone as a person and judging their actions. That is, even though the leaders may not approve of certain behaviors that a person exhibits, that does not mean that they dislike the person. This distinction was seldom, if ever, made by their parents; therefore, for the former victim, *doing* something wrong means one *is* wrong, or evil, and deserves abuse. Therefore, the process of correction must be handled gently and constructively.

In summary, even as group leaders attempt to be firm in maintaining group structure and encouraging members' growth, they must underscore that the decision to change is one that group members make for themselves. Leaders need to avoid even the appearance of authoritarian or controlling behavior. Still, they may be subjected to this charge. Most of the early experience that survivors of child abuse had with authority figures was autocratic and even brutal. Thus, many of their current experiences with authority figures are, correctly or incorrectly, perceived in the same light.

Being firm without at some time appearing controlling is a very delicate process and one in which no leader will succeed completely. Once again, true sensitivity to all the perceptions (even the incorrect ones) and fears of the group members, as well as careful analysis and gentle interpretation of the processes at work, must be combined with extreme patience to overcome this negative transference and challenge to the relationship.

❏ Serving as Role Models

In all of these efforts, the group leaders are called upon to be role models for the group members. Most abuse survivors have not had effective models in their lives. Not only were the relationships between them and their parents dysfunctional, but in most cases, the relationships their parents had with one another and with other adults were not healthy either.

The group leaders are therefore called upon to provide role models in many areas. Not only must they be the models of understanding, patience, emotional sensitivity, and the fair and unbiased authority we have just discussed, they also must be models for many social roles. They will often find themselves cast in the role of parent. They will, in fact, become surrogate parents at various times, being called upon to provide the care, support, and affirmation that the group members never received as children. At times, it will seem as if they are being asked to compensate for years of lost affection and nurturing. Even as that necessary parenting process goes on, the group members must be encouraged to find loving, supportive relationships with other members of the group and in their broader community as well as to learn ways to parent themselves and promote their own healing.

In addition, because the coleaders of the group are a woman and a man, they will be perceived as models of interpersonal, heterosexual relationships. The equality and respect they show one another may well be the first such relationship experienced by the group members. The degree to which they are able to share the leadership of the group and support and encourage one another will be an indication of the forms such relationships can take. The extent to which the group leaders can be comfortable with and relate well with one another will constantly communicate a variety of messages about male-female relationships. As the group leaders good-naturedly chide each other and offer support as well as criticism to one another, the group members will discover that male-female work relationships can be equal, satisfying, and productive. As the leaders affirm and complement each other's skills and strengths, these adults from dysfunctional families will experience the benefits of cooperative activity. They will encounter in concrete form the reality of mutual respect and appropriate interdependence.

❏ Summary

In short, all aspects of a group leader's life and personality will be called into play in working with a group for adult survivors. Such a task is not one that can be done half-heartedly and inattentively. The hypersensitivity and high expectations of former abuse victims do not allow for such an approach. But the rewards are great. Leaders develop a profound sense of awe as they experience in a concrete way the complex frailty, and yet tremendous resilience, of the human developmental process. They gain a new sense of faith in the healing power of the human spirit as they watch group members confront and conquer fears, accept new challenges, and take control over their previously shattered and scattered lives. They are affirmed in their belief that proper insight and guidance can overcome even the most devastating childhood.

6

Group Leader Self-Care

"My favorite activity after leading a survivor group—especially when the session has been pretty intense—is a good, hard game of squash. I take out my anger about what I have heard on that little black ball. It helps me clear out my head and my body."

—Jim, a 14-year veteran leader of survivor groups

"Working with adult survivors is really rewarding—they work so hard. But sometimes, hearing about the trauma gets to me. I really need to process some of those feelings with a colleague."

—Marie, after a year of coleading a group

One final commitment that a therapist or group leader needs to make when deciding to work with adult survivors is a pledge to self-care. As the professional literature reporting the incidence and effects of child abuse and neglect continues to grow, and as lay journalists print stories about the heroic struggles of adult survivors, the weight of carrying the "secret" has been lifted, and more and more survivors of abuse are seeking individual and group therapy to assist their recovery. Mental health professionals are now asking about the incidence of childhood abuse or neglect as a routine part of history taking, and the truth is coming out. As more and more clinicians begin to work with adult survivors, and as the traumatic events are shared directly or through dreams, flashbacks, and other dissociative states, we are beginning to see the occurrence of secondary posttraumatic stress disorder in therapists (Briere, 1989; Dolan, 1991). Sometimes, this is referred to as "vicarious" or "contact" victimization (Courtois, 1988; McCann & Pearlman, 1990).

Listening for several hours daily as terrified or enraged clients tell their stories and describe gruesome acts of physical violence, sexual cruelty, and emotional or psychological abuse perpetrated against small, innocent, and helpless children by adults who were entrusted with their care and protection certainly takes its toll emotionally and psychologically. This experience can change one's view of oneself and the world as well as undermine one's sense of safety, trust, self-esteem, independence, and power. It has even been known to interfere with a therapist's ability to be intimate with loved ones. Although working with adult survivors is challenging and tremendously rewarding, it is also extremely stressful.

Taking care of ourselves is critical not only for the effective treatment of our clients, but also for our own personal and professional health and well-being. We therapists need to fully recognize the high level of stress inherent in working with this population and carefully assess ourselves and our current situation in life to decide if this work is right for us. If the answer is "yes," the following suggestions hopefully will be useful in maintaining a healthy balance between work and personal life. Many of these strategies will be familiar because we frequently recommend them to clients for managing stress.

❏ Awareness of Stress Symptoms

Just as we help our clients to identify their own stress symptoms, we need to pay attention to the signs of stress in ourselves. Stress signs may be physical, emotional, or psychological. We need to watch for intermittent or unexplained aches and pains, especially in the neck or back. These may be caused by stress and tension (or lack of proper exercise). Headaches, sleep disturbances, and fatigue are also stress indicators. Loss of appetite, lack of enthusiasm for hobbies or social life, or diminished enthusiasm for work may all be signs of burnout. It is important to become aware of how stress affects us personally and changes our lives. Once our stress reactions are identified, we can act immediately to gain relief at the first signs of distress.

❏ Rest, Exercise, and Nutrition

We need to practice what we preach when encouraging clients to eat right, exercise, and be sure to get enough rest. Eating well-balanced meals and monitoring the amount of salt, sugar, and caffeine in our diet is necessary to maintaining good physical health and stable emotional status. Making exercise a routine part of our schedules and, if possible, including a spouse, friend, or colleague in this activity can help to ensure physical fitness. Keeping to a regular waking and sleeping schedule will help prevent fatigue and burnout.

Therapists are only human, and we often do not realize how stressed-out we are until we take an inventory of our caseload and find we are working 10 hours more per week than we had planned, and therefore, we are skipping lunch and dinner some days, we have dropped or modified our regular exercise plan, and we are too tired to do any of the fun things we used to enjoy. Doing a monthly or weekly assessment of how you spent your time can help you maintain a regular routine, and make necessary adjustments immediately if you get out of balance.

❏ Taking Time Off

We need to structure our schedules to include regular vacation times and "mental health" days to rejuvenate ourselves. To minimize the pressure or stress that these absences may create for clients, we can make a point of informing them several weeks in advance if we know that we will be away. One therapist who works with a large number of adult survivors gives them a tentative annual schedule that includes times that she knows she will be away on vacation or at conferences or speaking engagements. This enables them to plan in advance for her absence.

"Stay-at-home" vacations require forethought, too. Will we be available for emergencies, or will these be handled in some other way? Again, the boundaries and limits of availability need to be clearly stated to clients. Some therapists work together to provide "client emergency coverage" for each other when they are away. Such an arrangement provides support for clients and also allows the therapist to feel more free and easy about being away, especially for extended periods of time.

❏ Limits and Boundaries

A conscious decision about how many hours to work each week should be determined and maintained. Obviously, there needs to be some flexibility, but it is useful to keep within a certain set range. If the number of adult survivors in our caseload increases, it may be wise to work fewer hours per week because the level of emotional stress may rise as well. Therapists need to be aware that some survivors may require more than 1 hour per week; others may need telephone contact between appointments. This means that we need to consider carefully how many hours each day and evening we are willing and able to be available. A clear statement of our availability needs to be communicated to clients, and we also must be prepared to have it tested by some clients.

❏ Varying Our Caseloads

Many adult survivors spend several years in therapy as part of their recovery. In our experience, most have a year or more of individual work behind them before they venture into the group setting. We have found them to be hard-working and diligent clients, but their progress is often slow, painful, and plagued with depression. It is helpful to vary our caseloads to include clients whose therapy is less emotionally intense and does not involve resolution of trauma-based issues. Coleading a group for adult survivors can be a rewarding and less stressful substitute for 2 or 3 hours of individual therapy with these clients.

❏ Colleague Support and Consultation

Colleagues are invaluable sources of support and consultation. Setting up regular times to meet with each other to process our feelings about the work we are doing can be an effective way to give and receive helpful support. This is especially true if a therapist is in private practice alone. Some therapists develop informal "debriefing for mental health" groups where they commiserate with each other about the stresses and strains of mental health counseling. Others have established monthly "professional growth" groups where case studies are presented and treatment strategies are shared. There is still a lot to be learned about the treatment of trauma survivors, especially survivors of child abuse, and much may be gained by this type of collegial sharing. The ideas gained and the affirmation received from colleagues can be revitalizing both personally and professionally. Deciding to colead a group for adult survivors is another way to gain colleague support, one of the benefits that we have received from this work.

❑ Supervision

Another way to gain support is through formal or informal supervision by a more experienced clinician. Many group practices arrange weekly meetings where practitioners discuss cases and debrief one another. It is important to note, however, that being in a group practice does not guarantee regular collegial support. Being a therapist is inherently isolating because most time is spent one-on-one with clients. We need to take the initiative to ensure contact and provide support to each other, even within a group practice.

The regular debriefing sessions between coleaders of adult survivor groups can be an effective way of meeting each other's needs as well as gaining greater insights into the group process and progress of group members. Not only is the work of the group shared, but valuable professional support is gained. Some therapists who are new to leading these groups consult on a regular basis with someone who is more experienced.

❑ Countertransference

Effective handling of countertransference responses is important not only to the progress of the client, but also to the well-being of the therapist. As stated earlier, working with adult survivors of abuse requires that we listen to the horrible stories they tell of their childhoods; serve as witnesses to the intense pain and suffering they continue to experience; and deal repeatedly with their mistrust, testing, and manipulation. The stress involved in these tasks is almost guaranteed to arouse intense feelings within any therapist. These stories may elicit the same responses from the therapist that they do from the client, that is, denial, guilt, rage, dread, shame, and grief. We may be repulsed by the stories or fascinated to the point of voyeurism. We may be tempted to become a liberator or to extend our desire to help and nurture beyond appropriate professional boundaries.

More than any other client population, we need to be aware of how we are feeling as we work to assist in the recovery of these individuals. We need to monitor our own anger and outrage at the brutal treatment of innocent children and be careful that we do not overpower our clients with our emotional responses, which might be more intense than the clients' own reactions to the traumatic events. We recommend that countertransference issues be processed on a regular basis with a colleague or supervisor in order to maintain our own emotional balance and ensure good client care.

❑ Variety in Professional Activities

In addition to varying caseloads, we recommend that variety be added to professional activities. Teaching or taking classes and workshops, attending seminars and conferences, and collaborating on research with a colleague are productive ways to get a break from the rigors of a therapeutic practice. These activities provide a supportive milieu where professional growth may be enhanced. We also find it helpful to seek out opportunities for involvement in projects that promote or support a positive outlook on life and focus on acts of human kindness, because one of the negative side effects of working in the field of child abuse is exposure to large doses of inhumane and cruel acts.

❑ Spiritual Nurturing

Much of the recovery literature for adult survivors from dysfunctional families deals with spiritual issues. Many group leaders find that they learn a great deal about spirituality from group members.

Leehan (1993) has, in fact, written a book on sprirituality for survivors that has grown out of his experience in working with these groups. Often, group leaders are motivated to put energy into actively pursuing deeper spiritual growth and development as a way to counter the depleting aspects of helping others deal with trauma and its long-term effects. Engaging in prayer, yoga, or meditation activities can help us to become more in touch with our inner self and our higher power. Some therapists choose to examine the scriptures and writings of their faith tradition for teachings and resources that nurture the spiritual dimensions of their work. Others embark on their own faith or spiritual journeys and find this exploration to be a source of tremendous strength, power, and consolation. No matter what form it takes, a strong sense of connection to a basic life force is necessary if a therapist is going to sustain the hope required to work with this population. Such spiritual nurturing also enhances our therapeutic effectiveness. As we experience this growth and revitalization, both we and our clients will benefit.

❏ Separation of Private and Professional Lives

Finally, we emphasize the importance of keeping clear boundaries between personal and professional lives. It is easy to fall into the trap of bringing our work home or allowing it to encroach upon our private, personal time. Because of their strength, courage, and their undeniable right to a better life, abuse survivors are clients that pull on our need to provide care and support as helping professionals. But some of them may have needs that no single individual can ever satisfy, and we need to be careful that we do not try to give more than is healthy for ourselves and our families. Such overextension can result in the revictimization of a client when we are forced to pull back. The client may well experience this return to appropriate roles as abandonment or rejection. Thus, being clear about our limits and abilities is important not only for our own effective personal and professional functioning, but also for the well-being of our clients.

❑ Summary

In this chapter, we have emphasized the importance of therapist self-care for those who choose to work with adult survivors of childhood abuse. We have offered several suggestions for maintaining a healthy balance and a positive outlook on life. We trust that those who choose to lead these groups will be able to reap the benefits of this challenging but rewarding work and at the same time maintain a healthy lifestyle for themselves.

❑ Conclusion

The abuse of children has been a hidden reality in families since the beginning of human history. In its chronic forms, it creates an environment of familial fear that fills children with terror, helplessness, and mistrust. It generates chaos, isolation, and secrecy. It distorts victims' perceptions of the world, their relationships with others, and their own sense of identity.

To begin to support and treat these survivors of domestic violence is to open a Pandora's box of anger, pain, and confusion. It is an undertaking that requires skill, insight, strength, and, sometimes, infinite patience. And it is a task that can be both frightening and challenging, draining and exciting. There is probably no more demanding therapeutic task than providing abuse-focused therapy, especially within a group setting.

However, there is also no more rewarding form of therapy. Those who present themselves are those who have survived. They have experienced terrible pain and have endured. They have encountered horrendous violence and are seeking peace. They have been subjected to intense, unstable relationships, but they are committed to establishing meaningful bonds with others.

Although there is clearly a Pandora's crateful of hidden pain to be uncovered, there is an equally large portion of strength to be discovered. There is an enormous quantity of beauty, resilience, and faith in the face of adversity that can be revealed. Yes, those who have survived abuse have been victimized in dreadful ways, but they have managed to regain control over their chaotic lives. They have flourished even on rocky ground. Any form of therapy must help them to recognize and celebrate the strength that enabled them to create a new life different from what they experienced in their families.

Groups that bring survivors together to share, struggle, cry, laugh, curse, encourage, recognize, challenge, support, hug, blame, forgive, recall, accuse, open old wounds, and heal them again are a powerful way to address the needs of abused children who have grown up, but still have much to "grow out of." Such groups also can be a powerful experience for the therapists who lead them. The strength and commitment of the survivors can enrich the therapists' work, life, and faith. If you undertake this work, you will never be the same—you will be richer for it.

References

Agosta, C., & Loring, M. (1988). Understanding and treating the adult retrospective victim of child sexual abuse. In S. M. Sgroi (Ed.), *Vulnerable populations: Evaluation and treatment of sexually abused children and adult survivors* (Vol. 1, pp. 115-135). Lexington, MA: Lexington Books.

Bolton, F. G., Jr., Morris, L. A., & MacEachron, A. E. (1989). *Males at risk*. Newbury Park, CA: Sage.

Briere, J. (1989). *Therapy for adults molested as children: Beyond survival*. New York: Spring.

Briere, J. (1992). *Child abuse trauma*. Newbury Park, CA: Sage.

Browne, A., & Finkelhor, D. (1986). Impact of child sexual abuse: A review of the research. *Psychological Bulletin, 99*(1), 66-77.

Courtois, C. (1988). *Healing the incest wound: Adult survivors in therapy*. New York: Norton.

DeJong, A. R., Emmett, G. A., & Hervada, A. A. (1982). Epidemiologic factors in sexual abuse of boys. *American Journal of Diseases of Children, 136*, 990-993.

Dolan, Y. M. (1991). *Resolving sexual abuse: Solution-focused therapy and Ericksonian hypnosis for adult survivors*. New York: Norton.

Erikson, E. H. (1963). *Childhood and society*. New York: Norton.

Finkelhor, D. (1979). *Sexually victimized children*. New York: Free Press.

Finkelhor, D. (1988). The trauma of child sexual abuse: Two models. In G. A. Wyatt & G. J. Powell (Eds.), *Lasting effects of child sexual abuse* (pp. 61-82). Newbury Park, CA: Sage.

Finkelhor, D., & Browne, A. (1985). The traumatic impact of child sexual abuse: A conceptualization. *American Journal of Orthopsychiatry, 55,* 530-541.

Finkelhor, D., Hotaling, G., Lewis, I. A., & Smith, C. (1990). Sexual abuse in a national survey of adult men and women: Prevalence, characteristics, and risk factors. *Child Abuse & Neglect, 14,* 19-28.

Friedrich, W. N. (1990). *Psychotherapy of sexually abused children and their families.* New York: Norton.

Fritz, G. S., Stoll, K., & Wagner, N. A. (1981). A comparison of males and females who were sexually molested as children. *Journal of Sex and Marital Therapy, 7,* 54-59.

Gagnon, J. H. (1965). Female child victims of sex offenses. *Social Problems, 13,* 176-192.

Garbarino, J., & Gilliam, G. (1980). *Understanding abusive families.* Lexington, MA: D. C. Heath.

Garbarino, J., Guttman, E., & Seeley, J. (1986). *The psychologically battered child: Strategies for identification, assessment, and intervention.* San Francisco: Jossey-Bass.

Gelles, R. J. (1987). *Family violence.* Newbury Park, CA: Sage.

Gelles, R. J., & Cornell, C. P. (1985). *Intimate violence in families.* Newbury Park, CA: Sage.

Gil, E. (1988). *Treatment of adult survivors of child abuse.* Rockville, MD: Launch.

Hart, S. N., Germain, R., & Brassard, M. R. (1987). The challenge: To better understand and combat a psychological maltreatment of children and youth. In M. R. Brassard, R. Germain, & S. N. Hart (Eds.), *Psychological maltreatment of children and youth* (pp. 3-24). New York: Pergamon.

Helfer, R. E. (1978). *Childhood comes first: A crash course in childhood for adults.* East Lansing, MI: Author.

Herman, J. L. (1981). *Father-daughter incest.* Cambridge, MA: Harvard University Press.

Herman, J. (1992). *Trauma and recovery.* New York: Basic Books.

Jehu, D. (1988). *Beyond sexual abuse.* New York: Wiley.

Johnson, R., & Shrier, D. (1985, July 15). Massive effects on sex life of sex abuse of boys. *Sexuality Today, 8*(39), 1-2.

Justice, B., & Duncan, D. F. (1976). Life crisis as a precursor to child abuse. *Public Health Reports, 91,* 110-115.

Justice, B., & Justice, R. (1976). *The abusing family.* New York: Human Sciences Press.

Kempe, C. H., & Helfer, R. E. (1980). *The battered child.* Chicago: University of Chicago Press.

Kercher, G., & McShane, M. (1984). The prevalence of child sexual abuse victimization in an adult sample of Texas residents. *Child Abuse & Neglect, 8,* 485-502.

Leaman, K. M. (1980). Sexual abuse: The reactions of child and family. In *Sexual abuse of children: Selected readings* (pp. 21-24). Washington, DC: U.S. Department of Health and Human Services.

Leehan, J. (1993). *Defiant hope: Spirituality for survivors of family abuse.* Louisville, KY: Westminster/John Knox Press.

Leehan, J., & Wilson, L. P. (1985). *Grown-up abused children.* Springfield, IL: Charles C Thomas.

Lifton, R. J. (1979). *The broken connection.* New York: Simon and Schuster.

Maltz, W. (1991). *The sexual healing journey: A guide for survivors of sexual abuse.* New York: HarperCollins.

Maltz, W., & Holman, B. (1987). *Incest and sexuality.* Lexington, MA: Lexington Books.

Maslow, A. (1987). *Motivation and personality.* New York: Harper & Row.

McCann, I. L., & Pearlman, L. A. (1990). *Psychological trauma and the adult survivor: Theory, therapy, and transformation.* New York: Brunner/Mazel.

McCann, L., Pearlman, L. A., Sakheim, D. K., & Abrahamson, D. J. (1988). Assessment and treatment of the adult survivor of childhood sexual abuse within a schema framework. In S. M. Sgroi (Ed.), *Vulnerable populations: Evaluation and treatment of sexually abused children and adult survivors* (Vol. 1, pp. 77-101). Lexington, MA: Lexington Books.

McKay, M., & Paleg, K. (Eds.). (1992). *Focal group psychotherapy.* Oakland, CA: New Harbinger.

McWilliams, N. (1994). *Psychoanalytic diagnosis.* New York: Guilford.

Navarre, E. L. (1987). Psychological maltreatment: The core component of child abuse. In M. R. Brassard, R. Germain, & S. N. Hart (Eds.), *Psychological maltreatment of children and youth* (pp. 45-56). New York: Pergamon.

Nielsen, T. (1983). Sexual abuse of boys: Current perspectives. *Personnel and Guidance Journal, 62,* 139-142.

Russell, D. E. H. (1986). *The secret trauma: Incest in the lives of girls and women.* New York: Basic Books.

Sanford, L. T. (1990). *Strong at the broken places.* New York: Random House.

Seligman, M. E. P. (1975). *Helplessness: On depression, development, and death.* New York: Freeman.

Sgroi, S. M. (Ed.). (1988). *Vulnerable populations: Evaluation and treatment of sexually abused children and adult survivors, Vol. 1.* Lexington, MA: Lexington Books.

Smetana, J., Kelly, M., & Twentyman, C. (1984). Abused, neglected, and nonmaltreated children's judgments or moral and social transgressions. *Child Development, 55,* 277-287.

Sprei, J., with Unger, P. (1986). *A training manual for the group treatment of adults molested as children.* Rockville, MD: Montgomery County Sexual Assault Service.

Straus, M. A., Gelles, R. J., & Steinmetz, S. (1980). *Behind closed doors: Violence in the American family.* Garden City, NY: Doubleday/Anchor.

Summit, R. (1983). The child abuse accommodation syndrome. *Child Abuse & Neglect, 7,* 177-193.

van der Kolk, B. (1987). *Psychological trauma.* Washington, DC: American Psychiatric Press.

Vannicelli, M. (1989). *Group pyschotherapy with adult children of alcoholics: Treatment techniques and countertransference considerations.* New York: Guilford.

Webb, L. P. (1992). *PAST: People abused surviving together: An educational support group program for adult survivors of child abuse and neglect.* Cleveland, OH: Bellflower Center for Prevention of Child Abuse.

Westerlund, E. (1992). *Women's sexuality after childhood incest.* New York: Norton.

Wilson, J. P. (1980). Conflict, stress and growth. In C. R. Figley (Ed.), *Strangers at home* (pp. 123-165). New York: Praeger.

Wolfe, D. A. (1987). *Child abuse: Implications for child development and psychopathology.* Newbury Park, CA: Sage.

Wyatt, G. E., & Powell, G. J. (Eds.). (1988). *Lasting effects of child sexual abuse.* Newbury Park, CA: Sage.

Yalom, I. D. (1985). *The theory and practice of group psychotherapy.* New York: Basic Books.

Index

About the Authors

James Leehan, MA, MSSA, DMin, is an Episcopal priest and a Certified Social Worker and Marriage and Family Therapist who served as a campus minister for 25 years. In 1978, he began working with students abused as children. Since that time, he has continuously led groups for adult survivors of abuse; taught courses on domestic violence; and trained social workers, therapists, and clergy. The author of three other books—*Grown-Up Abused Children* (with Laura Pistone [Wilson] Webb), *Pastoral Care for Survivors of Family Abuse,* and *Defiant Hope: Spirituality for Survivors of Family Abuse*—Leehan is currently Affiliate Faculty at Christian Theological Seminary in Indianapolis, where he teaches and supervises students in the pastoral counseling and marriage and family therapy program. He is in private practice with Meridian Psychological Associates and conducts abuse prevention and healing seminars nationally. He and his wife, Melissa, lead retreats for survivors titled "Restoring Spirit, Mind, and Body."

Laura Pistone Webb, PhD, is a Licensed Professional Counselor in private practice in Cleveland, Ohio specializing in the treatment of adult survivors of child abuse and neglect. She began work in this area in 1980 as the coleader of a therapy group for "grown-up abused children" at Cleveland State University. While serving as Acting Program Director at the Bellflower Center for Prevention of Child Abuse, she developed a self-help group treatment program and authored the program manual, *PAST: People Abused Surviving Together: An Educational Support Group Program for Adult Survivors of Child Abuse and Neglect.* She also is coauthor (with James Leehan) of *Grown-Up Abused Children.* Her current focus is on writing and conducting training workshops on individual and group treatment of adult survivors.